The Psychology of Child Criminal Exploitation

Drawing on the narratives of adolescents and adults reflecting on their childhood experiences, this book offers a psychologically informed understanding of child criminal exploitation (CCE) as a dynamic, relational, and non-linear process.

Reflecting sustained empirical, theoretical, and practice-based engagement with CCE, the book moves beyond narrow risk factor approaches to examine how exploitation develops, becomes embedded, and, in some cases, is disrupted over time. It traces pathways from vulnerability and initiation through co-offending, emotional experience, identity formation, and desistance, highlighting the roles of coercion, constrained choice, social relationships, and structural inequalities.

Centring the voices of young people, the book challenges simplistic victim–offender binaries and explores how children understand, experience, and make sense of their involvement in exploitative contexts. By integrating forensic, developmental, social, and environmental psychology with contemporary criminological scholarship, it provides a process-oriented framework for understanding how exploitation is established, sustained, and resisted.

Offering important implications for safeguarding, youth justice, and professional practice, *The Psychology of Child Criminal Exploitation* will be of interest to students, researchers, practitioners, and policymakers working in psychology, criminology, youth justice, social care, education, and safeguarding.

Sally-Ann Ashton is an associate fellow of the British Psychological Society and is currently the director of the Center for Crime, Urban Research and Education (C-CURE) at the University of Houston-Downtown, Texas, USA.

Anna Bussu is a chartered psychologist (CPsychol), reader in criminal justice at Edge Hill University in the United Kingdom, and co-director of the Centre for Applied Criminal Justice and Policing Research.

Routledge Frontiers of Criminal Justice

Enabling Change in the Investigation of Rape and Serious Sexual Offending
Learning, Development and Wellbeing
Edited by Emma Williams

The Punitive Turn in Welfare State Sweden
Henrik Tham

Policing the Police
International Perspectives on Police Oversight
Erick Laming

Exploring the Impact of COVID-19 on Restorative Justice in Canada
Pandemic Justice
Muhammad Asadullah and Alana Abramson

Change Makers in Restorative Justice
The Transformative Power of Lived Experience
Allely Albert

Independent Police Accountability Bodies
Comparative Perspectives on Complaints Against the Police
Edited by Anja Johansen, Genevieve Lennon, Hartmut Aden, Christian Mouhanna, Marc Alain, and Tobias Singelnstein

The Psychology of Child Criminal Exploitation
From Initiation to Desistance
Sally-Ann Ashton and Anna Bussu

For more information about this series, please visit: www.routledge.com/Routledge-Frontiers-of-Criminal-Justice/book-series/RFCJ

The Psychology of Child Criminal Exploitation

From Initiation to Desistance

Sally-Ann Ashton and Anna Bussu

Routledge
Taylor & Francis Group
LONDON AND NEW YORK

First published 2027
by Routledge
4 Park Square, Milton Park, Abingdon, Oxon OX14 4RN

and by Routledge
605 Third Avenue, New York, NY 10158

Routledge is an imprint of the Taylor & Francis Group, an Informa business

British Library Cataloguing-in-Publication Data
A catalogue record for this book is available from the British Library

ISBN: 978-1-032-80370-8 (hbk)
ISBN: 978-1-032-80403-3 (pbk)
ISBN: 978-1-003-49669-4 (ebk)

DOI: 10.4324/9781003496694

Typeset in Times New Roman
by Apex CoVantage, LLC

Contents

Figures

Tables

About the authors

Sally-Ann Ashton is an associate fellow of the British Psychological Society and is currently the director of the Center for Crime, Urban Research and Education (C-CURE) at the University of Houston-Downtown, Texas, USA. She has an MPhil in criminological research (University of Cambridge, England) and an MSc in investigative psychology (University of Huddersfield, England). Her PhD explored the psychological and social risk factors associated with gang membership, group offending, and desistance from crime. She was a recipient of the National Gang Crime Research Center's Frederick Milton Thrasher Award in 2017 and 2024 for superior accomplishments in gang research and in 2020 for superior accomplishments in gang training. Her applied research continues to focus on gang prevention and response strategies, in addition to violent adolescent offending patterns. She is an international researcher and has published widely on group offending and child criminal exploitation. Her research focuses on the intersection between violence and psychological risk (reference to trauma, cognitive and personality development, and mental health), adolescent offending, community policing of vulnerable communities, and police legitimacy.

Anna Bussu is a reader in criminal justice at Edge Hill University, United Kingdom, and the co-director of the Centre for Applied Criminal Justice and Policing Research. She holds a PhD from the University of Sassari, Italy, with a dissertation in forensic psychology, and a master's degree in criminology from Sapienza University of Rome. She is a chartered Psychologist and senior fellow of the higher Education Academy. Her research sits at the intersection of criminal justice, forensic and social psychology, and youth justice, with a particular focus on child and adolescent vulnerability, early intervention, restorative and relational approaches, and the psychosocial factors associated with offending, victimisation, and desistance. Her work is strongly interdisciplinary and practice-oriented, combining psychological theory, qualitative and mixed-methods research, and applied engagement with criminal justice, safeguarding, and educational and community organisations. She has published widely on youth offending prevention, restorative justice, peer mentoring, cybervictimisation, and the social, emotional, and relational dimensions of young people's development. Her scholarship is underpinned by a commitment to child-centred, relational, and trauma-informed approaches that bridge research, policy, and professional practice.

Foreword

This important book aligns with my research and practice interests. I have published extensively on youth crime and justice, with my work appearing in leading international journals, including *Safer Communities*, *Probation Journal*, the *British Journal of Community Justice*, and the *Youth Justice Journal*. I recently contributed to an HM Inspectorate of Probation commissioned report on knowledge partnerships in youth justice, which examined how learning and evaluative cultures across youth justice services can be strengthened to support evidence-based and research-informed practice (Creaney & Price, 2025). I have also contributed to several edited collections, handbooks, and volumes, most notably in relation to desistance theory and participatory practice with children and young people in conflict with the law (Creaney et al., 2024).

What I have increasingly observed, and which resonates strongly with the themes explored in this book, is that the complexity of child criminal exploitation is still not fully recognised. At times, youth justice systems, processes, and responses do not properly acknowledge the structural, relational, and contextual dynamics that shape children's experiences (Ashton & Bussu, 2022; Robinson et al., 2018; Robinson, 2019). Understanding this complexity is important if we are to develop policies and practices that can genuinely protect and support children. These limitations can lead to misunderstandings and reinforce binary victim–perpetrator narratives, shaped by polarised thinking and a lack of contextual awareness (Ashton & Bussu, 2022; Robinson et al., 2018; Robinson, 2019). It is within this context that *The Psychology of Child Criminal Exploitation: From Initiation to Desistance* by Sally-Ann Ashton and Anna Bussu is an important and timely contribution to the field.

The authors integrate insights from criminology and psychology to explore how children can become victims of exploitation and how such involvement and contact with justice systems are sustained and, at times, disrupted. Their work adds new insights and contributes to contemporary debates by offering a psychologically informed account of exploitation that is grounded in empirical data and attentive to relational context.

This book demonstrates that justice-involved children are typically vulnerable in complex and overlapping ways. Many have experienced violence, abuse, poverty, inequality, and other forms of structural disadvantage. Children who have been coerced or forced into criminal activity—those who have been exploited—are particularly vulnerable, yet there can be difficulties identifying child victims and ensuring timely support.

My perspective on this book is shaped by research I have been involved in, which found that children assessed as "high-risk" of harm can become marginalised within adult-centric systems (Creaney & Burns, 2024; Hampson et al., 2024). They are not always consulted or meaningfully included in multi-agency high-risk panels, where limited understanding of the public protection, safeguarding, and risk management nexus persists. This can leave children feeling disempowered, reinforcing reductive victim–perpetrator binaries, especially when there is little opportunity for them to participate meaningfully in high-risk management processes (Creaney & Burns, 2025).

As Ashton and Bussu highlight in *The Psychology of Child Criminal Exploitation: From Initiation to Desistance*, justice-involved children typically face significant, complex challenges and issues. This insight is significant, as we still know relatively little about the lived experiences of children who have been exploited. This book is also important because the paucity of research in this area has created challenges for professionals within multi-agency teams, particularly when attempting to identify what works to promote positive outcomes for these children.

Safeguarding and community protection measures are necessary to keep child victims and communities safe, yet how such measures operate within a trauma-informed, child-centred framework remains under-explored. When children are absent from decision-making processes, or when there is little appetite to capture their experiences of victimisation or criminalisation, reductionist thinking can take hold, which may overlook the nuanced realities of their lives, leading to limited interpretations of risk, harm, and vulnerability.

The book brings together learning from relevant disciplines and integrates children's own accounts of exploitation. Drawing upon psychological theory, qualitative evidence, and practice-oriented insights, it offers an important new resource for academics, students, and policymakers. It will be particularly valuable for professionals working with vulnerable children across sectors such as youth justice, safeguarding, policing, education, and social care, where nuanced understanding of exploitation is important for effective practice.

Sean Creaney
Senior lecturer in criminal justice at
Edge Hill University

Sean Creaney (PhD) is a criminologist and senior lecturer in criminal justice, School of Law and Criminal Justice at Edge Hill University. Sean is a member of the Transdisciplinary Research for Youth Justice (TRYJustice) network. He recently co-edited *Knowledge and Skills Partnerships in Youth Justice*, which looks at the role of knowledge in enhancing youth justice practice.

References

Ashton, S.-A., & Bussu, A. (2022). Youth offending: An overview of the causes, implications and interventions. In S. Stanley (Ed.), *Contemporary social problems in the UK: A comprehensive overview* (pp. 147–167). Routledge. https://www.routledge.com/Contemporary-Social-Problems-in-the-UK-A-Comprehensive-Overview/Stanley/p/book/9780367764227

Creaney, S., & Burns, S. (2024). Freedom from symbolic violence? Facilitators and barriers to participatory practices in youth justice. *Youth Justice*, *24*(1), 31–52.

Creaney, S., & Burns, S. (2025). The Achilles heel of child first: High-risk panels in youth justice service policy and practice. *Probation Journal*, *0*(0). https://doi.org/10.1177/02645505251353719

Creaney, S., Burns, S., Douglas, A., Brierley, A., & Falconer, C. (2024). Desistance through participatory practice: Involving children in decision-making processes in youth justice. In A. Wigzell, C. Paterson-Young, & T. Bateman (Eds.), *Desistance and children*. Policy Press.

Creaney, S., & Price, J. (2025). *Knowledge partnerships in youth justice: Building learning and evaluative cultures*. HM Inspectorate of Probation Academic Insights 2025/06. https://hmiprobation.justiceinspectorates.gov.uk/document/knowledge-partnerships-in-youth-justicebuilding-learning-and-evaluative-cultures/

Hampson, K., Creaney, S., & Burns, S. (2024). Transforming the balance of power? Child first collaboration: A conceptual analysis. *Societies*, *14*(8), 138. https://doi.org/10.3390/soc14080138

Robinson, G. (2019). *Gangs, county lines and child criminal exploitation: A case study of Merseyside*. (Unpublished PhD thesis). Edge Hill University. https://research.edgehill.ac.uk/ws/portalfiles/portal/28769662/PhD

Robinson, G., McLean, R., & Densley, J. (2018). Working county lines: Child criminal exploitation and illicit drug dealing in Glasgow and Merseyside. *International Journal of Offender Therapy and Comparative Criminology*, *63*, 694–711. https://doi.org/10.1177/0306624X18806742

Acknowledgements

We would like to express our sincere gratitude to the children and adults who participated in and contributed to the research projects that have informed this book. We are deeply grateful for their time, trust, openness, and willingness to share their experiences. We also wish to thank the practitioners, professionals, and partner organisations who supported our research and helped us to better understand the complex realities of child criminal exploitation. Although our key partner organisation cannot be named, we are especially grateful for their support and assistance with finding participants for the two studies.

We are particularly grateful to Dr Sean Creaney for writing the Foreword to this book and for the thoughtful exchanges that helped us reflect on the importance of dialogue between criminology and psychology in understanding and supporting children affected by exploitation.

We are further grateful to our institutions—the Centre for Applied Criminal Justice and Policing Research at Edge Hill University and the Texas Juvenile Crime Prevention Center at Prairie View A&M University—for their support during the development and writing of this book.

Finally, we would like to thank our colleagues, families, friends, and our partners, Natham and Wil, for their encouragement, patience, and support throughout the writing process and for tolerating the many evenings, weekends, and conversations taken over by this book. Their humour, kindness, and steady support helped carry us through its most demanding stages.

Authors' note

This book was jointly conceived, developed, and written by both authors, who contributed equally to its conceptualisation, analysis, interpretation, writing, and revision. Authorship is presented in alphabetical order and should not be understood as reflecting any hierarchy of contribution.

Note on terminology

Throughout this book, the terms "child"/"children", "young person"/"young people", and "adolescent(s)" are occasionally used interchangeably to improve readability and avoid unnecessary repetition. We recognise that, in some contexts, the term "young people" may refer to a broader age range, often extending from approximately 13 to 25 years. However, unless otherwise specified, all references to children, young people, or adolescents in this book refer to individuals under the age of 18. References to adults refer to individuals aged 18 and over. In the analytical networks and tables, we consistently distinguish between young participants—those under 18—and adult participants—those aged 18 and over. The adult participants in the study reflected on their co-offending experiences before the age of 18.

Note on terminology

Introduction

Conceptualising child criminal exploitation as a dynamic and relational process

> A lot goes through your head at the moment, it's just wanting to get it over and done with because you get yourself stuck into a situation that you can only get out of, basically, but it's hard to get out of. You've got no one to tell, you don't want to tell anyone basically, you can't tell your mum because what's your mum going to do, you know she can't.
>
> (Young participant Y17)

I.1 Book structure and aims

Over the past decade, child criminal exploitation (CCE) has emerged as a central concern within youth justice, safeguarding, and criminal justice policy in the United Kingdom. Initially, it was framed predominantly through the lens of gangs and "county lines" drug trafficking. "County lines" refers to the dedicated mobile phone lines, or "[drug]deal lines", used by organised criminal networks to expand sales beyond larger cities into rural and coastal areas of the United Kingdom. More recently, CCE has increasingly been recognised as a complex form of child abuse involving coercion, manipulation, and constrained choice, particularly in relation to children's exploitation in the transportation and selling of drugs (HM Government, 2018).

The UK government has recently taken a significant step towards strengthening legal protections for children affected by CCE.[1] The Crime and Policing Act 2026 introduces a specific offence of CCE, recognising that children may be used, coerced, controlled, manipulated, or deceived by adults into criminal activity rather than acting as freely consenting participants. The act also introduces new offences relating to cuckooing, or home takeover, and internal concealment, reflecting growing legal recognition of the coercive and exploitative practices used by organised criminal groups. These developments align with the central argument of this book: that children involved in criminal exploitation should be understood through a safeguarding and victim-centred lens, rather than solely through criminal justice responses.

Despite this growing recognition, dominant policy and research approaches have tended to focus on observable outcomes, such as offending behaviour, arrest, or prosecution, rather than on the psychological, relational, and developmental

DOI: 10.4324/9781003496694-1

processes through which exploitation unfolds over time. Furthermore, a UK study found that professionals supporting criminally exploited children reported challenges in recognising children at risk and in understanding and managing the victim–perpetrator overlap that many present with. These challenges were exacerbated by the absence of a single statutory definition of CCE (Maxwell et al., 2026).

This book responds to this gap by advancing a process-oriented psychological framework for understanding CCE, tracing trajectories from pre-initiation and early involvement through to pathways of disengagement and desistance. Rather than treating CCE as a discrete event or a singular category of harm (Barlow et al., 2022), the book conceptualises exploitation as a dynamic and cumulative process shaped by early vulnerabilities, social relationships, emotional regulation, identity formation, and structural inequalities. From this perspective, CCE victimisation cannot be reduced to a one-off event with a simple or linear causal pathway, nor can victims be reliably identified through fixed lists of indicators or static "risk factors".

Instead, CCE must be conceptualised as a pattern of behaviours and experiences that emerge over time from the relational dynamics among children, motivated perpetrators, and the social environments they jointly inhabit (Barlow et al., 2022; Beckett & Warrington, 2014; Desai et al., 2002; Douglas et al., 2013; Finkelhor, 2008; Hart et al., 2003). At a basic level, CCE involves multiple actors, including the exploited child and the adults or older individuals who facilitate or perpetrate exploitation. As part of the exploitation, children are coerced or forced into performing criminal acts. In this sense, the book challenges binary distinctions between "victim" and "offender" and foregrounds children's lived experiences within contexts of coercion, dependency, and limited alternatives.

Children affected by CCE do not readily adhere to fixed or uniform profiles. Rather, they are more appropriately understood as occupying positions of heightened vulnerability arising from the interplay of individual experiences, relational contexts, and broader structural conditions. Existing research has highlighted the significance of adverse childhood experiences (ACEs), family instability, and exposure to trauma in shaping susceptibility to harm (Felitti et al., 1998; Finkelhor, 2008; van der Kolk, 2014). However, such factors should be conceptualised as contributing to conditions of vulnerability rather than as direct or deterministic causes of exploitation.

Ashton (2023) identified two distinct entry points for exploitation by organised criminal groups. The first scenario arises when a child is approached by a stranger acting as a recruiter for a criminal group, who either recognises the young person as vulnerable or assesses their openness through the offer of financial incentives. In other cases, exploitation emerges through existing social relationships with peers, family members, or older individuals who may initially be perceived as sources of support, protection, or opportunity (Ashton, 2025). Within these contexts, early engagement is not necessarily experienced as coercive or exploitative. Instead, it may be understood as part of everyday social interaction, learning, or adaptation to local environments, particularly where access to legitimate opportunities is constrained (Densley, 2013; Wikström et al., 2012). Over time, however, these relational dynamics typically become increasingly characterised by dependency, obligation, and control. Coercion within CCE is not always immediate or explicit but may develop gradually through processes of trust-building, expectation, and the normalisation of harmful practices. From this perspective, children's actions are more accurately interpreted as occurring within conditions of constrained choice, where agency remains present but significantly constrained by unequal power relations and restricted alternatives (HM Government, 2018).

A further complexity lies in how children themselves interpret their involvement. Many do not readily identify as victims and may instead describe their participation in terms of necessity, loyalty, or personal responsibility. Such accounts point to the limitations of binary victim–offender distinctions, which risk obscuring the relational and coercive dimensions of exploitation (Barlow et al., 2022). Young people's narratives often reflect attempts to make sense of their circumstances within environments characterised by uncertainty, risk, and constraint (Ashton, 2023).

These experiences are also situated within wider structural and environmental contexts. Social disadvantage, educational exclusion, and neighbourhood-level deprivation may both increase exposure to exploitative networks and limit opportunities for disengagement. In this sense, CCE may be understood not solely as an issue of individual behaviour but as one embedded within broader patterns of inequality and social harm (Desai et al., 2002; Douglas et al., 2013; Hart et al., 2003).

All these considerations suggest that the characteristics of children experiencing criminal exploitation are best understood through a relational and process-oriented lens. Such an approach foregrounds the ways in which vulnerability is produced and reproduced over time through the interaction of personal histories, social relationships, and structural constraints (Ashton, 2023). This perspective provides an important foundation for the analysis that follows, particularly in relation to coercion, control, and constrained choice.

Drawing on cognitive, developmental, environmental, forensic, and social psychological perspectives, this book integrates insights from criminology and psychology to explore how children become involved in criminal activity with family members, peers, and older offenders and how such involvement is normalised, sustained, and at times disrupted. Existing research has consistently highlighted the role of ACEs, family adversity, school exclusion, neighbourhood deprivation, and antisocial peer networks in shaping vulnerability to exploitation (Densley, 2012, 2023; Felitti et al., 1998; Hesketh & Robinson, 2019). However, less attention has been paid to how these risk factors are experienced psychologically, interpreted, and narrated by children themselves.

This book addresses that omission by *centring the voices* of those who have experienced criminal exploitation. It examines not only *what* children do, but also *how they understand their actions*, *how they regulate emotions under coercive conditions*, and *how identities are constructed and renegotiated* across time. In doing so, the book contributes to contemporary debates on safeguarding and desistance by offering a psychologically informed account of exploitation that is grounded in empirical data and attentive to relational context.

The book is organised into five chapters and a conclusion, each addressing a distinct but interconnected dimension of CCE.

Chapter 1—From Vulnerability to Exploitation: this chapter introduces a process-oriented framework for understanding early stages of CCE. It conceptualises exploitation as a relational and psychological process rather than a discrete event, highlighting how vulnerability emerges through familial experiences, structural disadvantage, relational adversity, and individual factors. The chapter examines coercion, constrained choice, and early psychological conditioning dynamics, introducing analytical networks that map risk factors and exploitative processes. It establishes early identification and child-first intervention as critical opportunities for disrupting exploitation trajectories.

Chapter 2—Co-offending roles, training, and progression: this chapter examines how children become embedded in criminal activity through co-offending, training, and role progression within criminal groups. Integrating Bronfenbrenner's ecological systems theory with contextual safeguarding, routine activities theory, rational choice theory, and social learning theory, the chapter explores how individual vulnerabilities, relational dynamics, peer and family influences, and situational opportunities interact to shape involvement in CCE. It examines impulsive and planned offending, shifting co-offending roles, and the transmission of criminal skills by peers, family members, and older offenders. The chapter highlights how training, testing, and loyalty reinforce dependency, constrain exit, and contribute to escalation and entrenchment within exploitative networks. Particular attention is given to the relational and environmental conditions through which offending behaviours become normalised, reinforced, and sustained over time.

Chapter 3—Emotions and offending experiences: this chapter foregrounds emotions as central mechanisms in the criminal exploitation of children. It analyses emotional experiences during the orchestration of a crime, at the point of arrest, and after offending, demonstrating how emotions such as excitement, emotional numbing, fear, guilt, and relief both sustain and disrupt exploitation. Emotional suppression is interpreted as an adaptive response to coercion, while negative emotions and arrest-related relief are identified as potential moments of rupture and intervention within exploitation trajectories. The chapter further demonstrates how emotional regulation within exploitative contexts may function simultaneously as a survival strategy and a mechanism sustaining continued criminal involvement.

Chapter 4—Self-perception and self-awareness: this chapter examines identity, self-perception, and self-awareness within contexts of constrained agency. It shows how repeated criminal involvement and exposure to violence can shape self-perceptions of competence, status, and maturity, even where exploitation is present. Building on the emotional dynamics explored in the previous chapter, the analysis demonstrates how exploitative relationships and offending experiences can contribute to the formation of antisocial identities. Reflective self-awareness often emerges retrospectively, particularly following emotional rupture or separation from exploitative peers. The chapter highlights identity change as fragile, relational, and non-linear, challenging simplistic victim–offender binaries.

Chapter 5—Pathways to desistance: this chapter conceptualises desistance from CCE as a non-linear, relational, and supported process. Building on earlier chapters, it examines how rupture (release from the group), identity reflection, and external disruption can initiate disengagement, while ongoing coercion and structural constraints limit choice. The proposed *Exploitation–Desistance Journey in Child Criminal Exploitation* (Figure 5.2) traces movement from initiation to entrenchment, rupture, and desistance, highlighting that cessation is fragile and contingent on support. Emotional rupture and reflective self-awareness emerge as critical intervention points. The findings challenge punitive and risk-led responses, advocating instead for trauma-informed and relational approaches. The chapter emphasises that sustainable desistance depends on child-centred, trauma-informed, and multi-agency support rather than disruption or punishment alone. It further argues that meaningful opportunities for safety, belonging, and identity reconstruction are essential for sustaining long-term disengagement from exploitative networks.

Chapter 6—Conclusions: the book concludes that CCE is best understood as a dynamic and non-linear process shaped by vulnerability, coercion, emotional regulation, and constrained choice. Exploitation frequently unfolds through relational and emotionally embedded pathways that obscure its recognition as harm. Building on the desistance pathway discussed in Chapter 5, the *Child Criminal Exploitation Desistance Model* (Figure 6.2) presented in Chapter 6 distinguishes between release from coercive control and desistance from offending behaviour, emphasising that leaving an exploitative group does not automatically equate to recovery, restored agency, or the cessation of crime. Sustainable desistance, therefore, requires early identification, multi-agency collaboration, relational safety, and meaningful alternatives to criminal involvement. Overall, the book argues for a process-oriented and relational understanding of CCE capable of recognising both children's vulnerabilities and the complex constraints shaping their pathways into and out of exploitation.

The overarching aim of this book is to advance understanding of CCE in order to support *early identification, prevention, and child-centred intervention.*

By integrating psychological theory, qualitative evidence, and practice-oriented insights, the book is intended for academics, students, practitioners, policymakers, and professionals working across youth justice, safeguarding, policing, education, and social care. By foregrounding children's voices and situating their experiences within relational and structural contexts, this volume seeks to move beyond punitive or reductionist responses and contribute to more humane, effective, and psychologically informed approaches to addressing the criminal exploitation of children.

The book centres the voices of survivors of exploitation by tracing pathways from heightened social and environmental vulnerability to the psychological, structural, and relational origins of exploitation (Chapter 1). It then examines psychological conditioning, criminal training, and embeddedness as processes that lay the foundations for criminal exploitation (Chapter 2). The book subsequently considers the diverse range of emotions reported by children affected by exploitation, exploring emotional mechanisms that may sustain or disrupt coercive control (Chapter 3). It then examines changes in self-perception and self-awareness, showing how retrospective reflection may contribute to new forms of identity formation (Chapter 4). Finally, desistance (Chapter 5) is presented as a non-linear process that can generate heightened vulnerabilities for children and requires relational support as survivors rebuild their identities and lives.

This narrative progression is synthesised in Figure I.1, which illustrates how the book traces CCE as a movement from vulnerability and exploitation through conditioning, emotional experience, identity change, and supported desistance (see Figure I.1).

Adult participant A21 provides a case study illustrating this process, demonstrating how vulnerability, co-offending, exposure to organised criminal groups, arrest, self-reflection, and desistance unfold across the life course. His first offence,

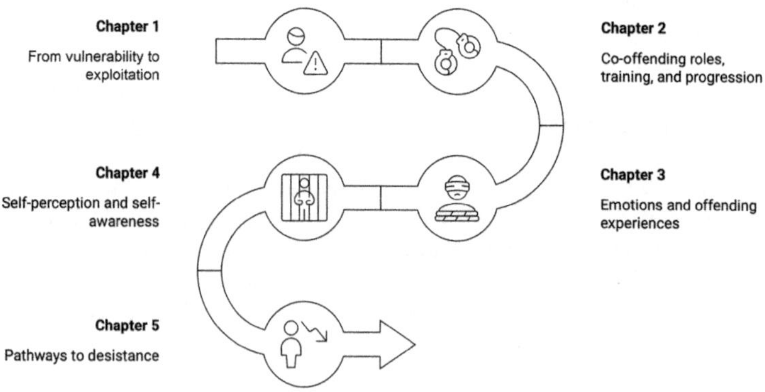

Figure I.1 Diagram showing the book narrative

criminal damage, occurred at the age of 12. Between the ages of 12 and 17, he exhibited antisocial behaviours, sensory and thrill-seeking activities, reactive violent offending, and income-generating offences and began using illegal substances, including cannabis, cocaine, and amphetamines after the age of 15 (see Table I.1). His offending comprised solo offending and co-offending with peers and with older criminals who were part of an organised crime group and who lived locally. There was no family history of criminal justice involvement. He reported one adverse childhood experience, witnessing his mother being beaten. During the interview, he described the offence as armed robbery carried out with two members of an organised criminal group who were 5 or 6 years older than him at a time when he was 16 years old. His vulnerabilities included behavioural factors (substance use and lack of impulse control), social factors (antisocial peers and exposure to adult criminal gangs), and environmental elements (poverty and access to criminal groups locally). He described himself as "a product of his environment" and as someone who has learnt "behaviours from older people". He recalled how he had initiated contact with the group:

> I started doing things, trying to give myself a name, just for me to get noticed by them. And I was always trying to be in that area where they was, er . . . be at house parties where they was and then I just . . . sort of like got in there, do you know what I mean, slowly but surely.

Participant A21 was recruited into an armed robbery as part of a wider team and assigned a relatively minor role, which he described as learning through direct participation. He reported feeling initially nervous, followed by a sense of exhilaration both during the commission of the offence and afterwards upon

Table I.1 Case study A21: offending history before the age of 18 years

Offence	*Alone*	*With peers*	*With older*
Arson	YES	YES	YES
Antisocial behaviour	YES	YES	YES
Criminal damage	YES	NO	NO
Assault	YES	YES	YES
Fighting	YES	YES	YES
Carrying a weapon	YES	YES	YES
Carjacking	YES	YES	YES
Theft of motor vehicle	YES	NO	NO
Theft of property	YES	YES	YES
Joyriding	YES	NO	NO
Possession of controlled drug "A"*	YES	NO	NO
Possession of controlled drug "B"*	YES	NO	NO

* In England, drugs are classified according to the Misuse of Drugs Act 1971. Class A drugs are considered the most harmful (e.g., heroin, cocaine, and ecstasy), and Class B drugs are considered less harmful (e.g., cannabis, ketamine, and amphetamines).

receiving a substantial financial payment. Following his arrest and conviction, his self-perception shifted significantly. Midway through serving an eight-year sentence, his wife divorced him, prompting a period of reflection during which he recognised the need to change. This marked the beginning of his engagement with education in prison, where he undertook training and later worked as a mentor. At the time of the interview, he was running his own non-profit business helping formerly incarcerated individuals reintegrate into their communities.

A similar pattern was evident among the child participants in the study. Participants Y1, Y6, Y15, and Y17 had been recruited by organised criminal groups and trafficked to sell drugs on their behalf. At the time of their interviews, three of these children had been arrested, an experience that enabled them to break free from their exploiters and obtain support. One participant, however, was still embedded within the group that was exploiting him and, like A21 when he was a child, struggled to recognise his situation as exploitative. The chapters highlight shared aspects of participants' experiences while also delineating key differences in vulnerabilities, the nature of exploitation, their awareness of the process, and their trajectories towards desistance.

I.2 An evidence-based, process-oriented approach

I.2.1 Research aims, design, and methodology

The primary aim of our research underpinning this book is to generate an evidence-based, process-oriented understanding of CCE, recognising its complexity as a multifaceted and evolving phenomenon within contemporary youth justice and safeguarding contexts (Maxwell et al., 2019; Maxwell, 2024). Specifically, our book examines how exploitation is experienced, interpreted, and navigated across different stages, from initiation to desistance. In line with emerging literature, CCE is conceptualised not as a linear or discrete event but as a dynamic and relational process shaped by the interaction among individuals, environments, and exploitative networks (Barlow et al., 2022).

Rather than testing predefined hypotheses, this research seeks to illuminate the psychological, emotional, relational, and identity-based processes that underpin children's involvement in, and disengagement from, criminal exploitation. This approach reflects recent scholarship emphasising the importance of understanding how victimhood, agency, and identity are constructed and negotiated through social interactions and institutional responses (Marshall, 2024; Dando et al., 2023). Each chapter is therefore structured around empirical findings derived from the same mixed-methods datasets and analytical approach. The inclusion of research aims, methodology, and data analysis within the introduction reflects the consistency of the research design across the book. Empirical findings provide the starting point for each chapter. These inform the relevant theoretical frameworks to interpret the results and to develop targeted, evidence-informed implications for policy, safeguarding, and professional practice. Overall, this book adopts an evidence-based qualitative approach, in which empirical findings systematically inform theoretical interpretation and the development of policy and practice implications.

I.2.2 Research design and procedures

The book is underpinned by two complementary qualitative datasets collected in England, generating a sample of 32 individuals. The first comprises interviews with 20 adolescent males, aged 14 to 17, who had been involved in a community intervention for violence and/or gang-related activity in the North West of England (Ashton, 2023; Ashton & Bussu, 2020, 2023). These interviews explored experiences of co-offending with peers, exposure to older offenders, emotional responses during and after offending, and perceptions of agency and choice.

The second dataset consists of 12 interviews with adult males aged between 27 and 64 at the time of the interview who reflected retrospectively on crimes committed between the ages of 13 and 17 in the presence of at least one older co-offender. This second sample enabled a longitudinal and reflective perspective on exploitation, identity, and desistance. The research used semi-structured interviews in which participants were asked to share an experience of co-offending and/or to describe a criminal act that occurred in the presence of at least one other person who was older (Ashton & Bussu, 2023).

Both samples were asked to report their offending behaviours during adolescence, and these data were triangulated with police records and intelligence for the children. The adult interviewees were also asked to complete an expanded adverse childhood experiences (ACEs) questionnaire based on the original CDC–Kaiser ACE questionnaire (Felitti et al., 1998), supplemented with additional indicators commonly used in expanded and urban ACEs studies to capture family instability, system involvement, and severe loss (see Cronholm et al., 2015).

The study was informed by *Social Identity Theory* (Tajfel & Turner, 1979; Turner, 1987), which provides a critical framework for understanding how group membership, status, and belonging shape behaviour and self-concept within exploitative contexts (Ellemers & Haslam, 2012). This was complemented by *ecological and developmental perspectives* that situate individual experiences within wider social systems, including family, peers, schools, neighbourhoods, and structural inequality (Bronfenbrenner, 1979). According to Ellemers and Haslam (2012, p. 379), "The [social identity] theory argues that social identity underpins intergroup behaviour and sees this as qualitatively distinct from interpersonal behavior".

I.2.3 Data analysis

A qualitative methodological approach was employed to explore in depth how experiences of CCE were understood, narrated, and made sense of by participants. This approach was considered particularly appropriate for capturing the complexity of lived experiences and the emotional, relational, and contextual factors shaping pathways into, through, and away from criminal exploitation.

The dataset consisted of face-to-face semi-structured interviews conducted with children who had experienced CCE, alongside adults reflecting retrospectively on their earlier involvement. All interviews were audio-recorded and transcribed verbatim before analysis. Data were analysed thematically using ATLAS.ti (version 26.0) to support systematic coding, data management, and interpretive analysis.

Thematic analysis, following the reflexive approach outlined by Braun and Clarke (2019, 2024a, 2024b, 2024c), provided a flexible yet rigorous analytical framework for identifying patterns of meaning across participants' accounts while remaining sensitive to individual trajectories and contextual variation. Particular attention was paid to participants' subjective experiences, emotional responses, relational dynamics, and perceptions of agency, vulnerability, and change across different stages of exploitation.

Coding was conducted inductively, allowing themes to emerge directly from the data rather than being imposed through a pre-existing theoretical framework. The analytic process was iterative and interpretive, involving repeated engagement with the transcripts and ongoing refinement of codes to ensure that they accurately reflected participants' meanings. Coding was undertaken manually by two researchers, with ATLAS.ti used to organise codes, track analytic decisions, and support reflexive engagement with the data.

ATLAS.ti's visualisation tools were used to explore relationships between codes and to map connections across themes, supporting the development of a nuanced and process-oriented understanding of participants' experiences. This facilitated the identification of shared patterns as well as variations in emotional responses, trajectories of involvement, and moments of reflection or change.

The analysis was guided by established criteria for rigour in qualitative research (Seale, 1999), with particular emphasis placed on analytic transparency, reflexivity, and credibility. Care was taken to ensure that participants' accounts were represented authentically and that interpretations remained grounded in the data, recognising both the sensitivity of the subject matter and the ethical responsibilities involved in research with exploited and formerly exploited individuals.

During the interviews with adult participants, it became apparent that ACEs and family relational difficulties influenced their adolescent behaviours and increased their vulnerabilities to exploitation. For this reason, we conducted a multidimensional scaling analysis to understand the relationship between these variables for the second sample. The adult interviews were dichotomously coded as present or absent according to offence type, relationship to co-offender, and age of co-offender. These data were then analysed using "*Smallest Space Analysis* (SSA-I; Lingoes, 1973), an established multidimensional scaling procedure that shows the relationship of every variable to every other variable. Each variable is plotted as a spatial representation showing the associated correlations between them" (Ashton et al., 2021, 1040). Although the book is grounded in UK-based research data, its significance has the potential to extend beyond the United Kingdom through its engagement with international evidence and frameworks on CCE and youth justice. By analysing processes such as recruitment, coercion, constrained choice, the victim–offender overlap, and criminalisation, the book addresses challenges faced by youth justice systems in the United Kingdom but has international relevance.

Note

1 https://www.gov.uk/government/publications/crime-and-policing-act-2026-factsheets/crime-and-policing-act-2026-child-criminal-exploitation-cuckooing-home-takeover-and-internal-concealment-factsheet

References

Ashton, S. A. (2023). *Pathways to adolescent male violent offending*. Routledge.

Ashton, S. A. (2025). A geography of early vulnerabilities and exploitation in the narratives of adolescent males in England. *Journal of Criminal Psychology*, *15*(1), 55–71. https://doi.org/10.1108/JCP-07-2024-0064

Ashton, S. A., & Bussu, A. (2020). Peer groups, street gangs and organised crime in the narratives of adolescent male offenders. *Journal of Criminal Psychology*, *10*(4), 277–292. https://doi.org/10.1108/JCP-06-2020-0020

Ashton, S. A., & Bussu, A. (2023). The social dynamics of adolescent co-offending. *Youth Justice*, *23*(3), 350–371. https://doi.org/10.1177/14732254221136044

Ashton, S. A., Valentine, M., & Chan, B. (2021). *Differentiating Categories of Violent Adolescent Offending and the Associated Risks in Police and Youth Offending Service Records*. https://doi.org/10.1177/0306624x211058960

Barlow, C., Kidd, A., Green, S. T., & Darby, B. (2022). Circles of analysis: A systemic model of child criminal exploitation. *Journal of Children's Services*, *17*(3), 158–174. https://doi.org/10.1108/JCS-04-2021-0016

Beckett, H., & Warrington, C. (2014). *Suffering in silence: Children and unreported crime*. University of Bedfordshire.

Braun, V., & Clarke, V. (2019). Reflecting on reflexive thematic analysis. *Qualitative Research in Sport, Exercise and Health*, *11*, 589–597. https://doi.org/10.1080/2159676X.2019.1628806

Braun, V., & Clarke, V. (2024a). Reporting guidelines for qualitative research: A values-based approach. *Qualitative Research in Psychology*, *22*(2), 399–438. https://doi.org/10.1080/14780887.2024.2382244

Braun, V., & Clarke, V. (2024b). A critical review of the reporting of reflexive thematic analysis in *Health Promotion International*, *39*(3), daae049. https://doi.org/10.1093/heapro/daae049

Braun, V., & Clarke, V. (2024c). Supporting best practice in reflexive thematic analysis reporting in Palliative Medicine: A review of published research and introduction to the Reflexive Thematic Analysis Reporting

Guidelines (RTARG). *Palliative Medicine, 38*(6), 608–616. https://doi.org/10.1177/0269216324123480

Bronfenbrenner, U. (1979). *The ecology of human development: Experiments by nature and design*. Harvard University Press.

Cronholm, P. F., Forke, C. M., Wade, R., Bair-Merritt, M. H., Davis, M., Harkins-Schwarz, M., Pachter, L. M., & Fein, J. A. (2015). Adverse childhood experiences: Expanding the concept of adversity. *American Journal of Preventive Medicine, 49*(3), 354–361. https://doi.org/10.1016/j.amepre.2015.02.001

Dando, C. J., Ormerod, T. C., & Atkinson-Sheppard, S. (2023). Parental experiences of the impact of grooming and criminal exploitation of children for county lines drug trafficking. *Journal of Public Health, 45*(2), e346–e354.

Densley, J. (2012). The organisation of London's street gangs. *Global Crime, 13*(1), 42–64. https://doi.org/10.1080/17440572.2011.632497

Densley, J. A. (2013). *How gangs work: An ethnography of youth violence*. Basingstoke: Palgrave Macmillan.

Densley, J. A., McLean, R., & Brick, C. (2023). *Contesting county lines: Case studies in drug crime and deviant entrepreneurship*. Bristol University Press.

Desai, S., Arias, I., Thompson, M. P., & Basile, K. C. (2002). Childhood victimization and subsequent adult revictimization assessed in a nationally representative sample of women and men. *Violence and Victims, 17*(6), 639–653. https://doi.org/10.1891/vivi.17.6.639.33725

Douglas, K. S., Hart, S. D., Webster, C. D., & Belfrage, H. (2013). *HCR-20 (Version 3): Assessing risk for violence—User guide*. Mental Health, Law and Policy Institute, Simon Fraser University.

Ellemers, N., & Haslam, S. A. (2012). Social identity theory. In P. A. M. Van Lange, A. W. Kruglanski, & E. T. Higgins (Eds.), *Handbook of theories of social psychology* (Vol. 2, pp. 379–398). Sage.

Felitti, V. J., Anda, R. F., Nordenberg, D., Williamson, D. F., Spitz, A. M., Edwards, V., et al. (1998). Relationship of childhood abuse and household dysfunction to many of the leading causes of death in adults: The Adverse Childhood Experiences (ACE) study. *American Journal of Preventative Medicine, 14*(4), 245–258. https://doi.org/10.1016/S0749-3797(98)00017-8

Finkelhor, D. (2008). *Childhood victimization: Violence, crime, and abuse in the lives of young people*. Oxford University Press.

Hart, S. D., Kropp, R., Laws, D. R., Klaver, J., Logan, C., & Watt, K. A. (2003). *The Risk for Sexual Violence Protocol (RSVP): Structured Professional Guidelines for Assessing Risk of Sexual Violence*. Mental Health, Law, and Policy Institute, Simon Fraser University.

Hesketh, R. F., & Robinson, G. (2019). Grafting: "The boyz" just doing business? Deviant entrepreneurship in street gangs. *Safer Communities, 18*(2), 54–63. https://doi.org/10.1108/SC-05-2019-0016

HM Government. (2018). *Serious violence strategy*. https://www.gov.uk/government/publications/serious-violence-strategy

Marshall, H. (2024). Child criminal exploitation and the interactional emergence of victim status. *The British Journal of Criminology, 64*(5), 1011–1027. https://doi.org/10.1093/bjc/azae008

Maxwell, N. (2024). *Child criminal exploitation.* (Academic Insights 2024/04). HM Inspectorate of Probation.

Maxwell, N., Khurana, K., & Cserző, D. (2026). 'They're not seeing young people as victims': Professional perspectives on policy and practice for criminally exploited children in Wales. *Youth Justice*, *0*(0). https://doi.org/10.1177/14732254261428267

Maxwell, N., Wallace, C., Cummings, A., Bayfield, H., & Morgan, H. (2019). *A systematic map and synthesis review of child criminal exploitation.* CASCADE, Cardiff University.

Seale, C. (1999). Quality in qualitative research. *Qualitative Inquiry*, *5*(4), 465–478.

Tajfel, H., & Turner, J. C. (1979). An integrative theory of intergroup conflict. In W. G. Austin & S. Worchel (Eds.), *The social psychology of intergroup relations* (pp. 33–47). Brooks/Cole.

Turner, J. C. (1987). A self-categorization theory. In J. C. Turner, M. A. Hogg, P. J. Oakes, S. D. Reicher, & M. S. Wetherell (Eds.), *Rediscovering the social group: A self-categorization theory* (pp. 42–67). Blackwell.

van der Kolk, B. (2014). *The body keeps the score: Brain, mind, and body in the healing of trauma*. Viking.

Wikström, P.-O. H., Oberwittler, D., Treiber, K., & Hardie, B. (2012). *Breaking rules: The social and situational dynamics of young people's urban crime*. Oxford University Press.

1 From vulnerability to exploitation

A process-oriented framework for early child criminal exploitation

1.1 Introduction

1.1.1 Introduction and definition of child criminal exploitation in its early stages

Child criminal exploitation (CCE) has emerged in recent years as a central concept within youth justice in the United Kingdom, reflecting a significant shift in how children involved in offending behaviours are understood and responded to. At its core, CCE challenges traditional binaries between "offender" and "victim" by recognising that children may be drawn into criminal activity through processes of coercion, manipulation, and abuse, often long before their involvement becomes visible to statutory systems (Marshall, 2024; Maxwell, 2024). While the concept has gained prominence in the UK policy landscape, it is increasingly situated within international debates concerning child exploitation, organised crime, and youth vulnerability (Barlow et al., 2022; Maxwell et al., 2019). While legal definitions are essential for determining responsibility, thresholds of intervention, and statutory duties, they do not fully capture the psychological processes through which exploitation unfolds, particularly in its early stages. This distinction is critical, as the lived experiences of exploited children frequently diverge from the categories through which systems seek to identify and respond to harm. From a legal perspective, CCE is typically defined through observable acts: coercion, control, manipulation, and involvement in criminal activity for the benefit of others (Home Office, 2018; Maxwell, 2024). Legal frameworks are necessarily event-focused and outcome-oriented, relying on evidence that exploitation has occurred or that a child has been involved in criminal behaviour. By contrast, from a psychological and developmental perspective, CCE is best understood as a process, often gradual and relational, embedded within grooming dynamics, emotional dependency, and constrained choice.

Psychologically, early-stage exploitation, as reflected in traditional definitions of CCE, is often assumed to involve explicit coercion, threats, or violence. However, this framing risks obscuring the earlier and more subtle

DOI: 10.4324/9781003496694-2

stages through which exploitation develops. In contrast, this study adopts a broader, process-oriented perspective, recognising that early-stage exploitation rarely begins with overt force (Ashton, 2023). Instead, it frequently develops through perceived friendship, protection, reciprocity, or belonging (Dando et al., 2023; Maxwell et al., 2019). Children may experience a sense of agency, loyalty, or status within these relationships, even as exploitative control is being established. This creates a significant tension between legal definitions, which may rely on clear indicators of coercion, and children's subjective experiences, which may not align with notions of victimhood or abuse (Marshall, 2024). This conceptual gap has important implications. Children may not recognise themselves as exploited, may actively resist intervention, or may present behaviours that are interpreted by professionals as wilful offending rather than as responses to coercive circumstances (Marshall, 2024). As a result, a narrow reliance on legal definitions risks obscuring early exploitation and reinforcing criminalising responses, particularly where psychological harm precedes legally recognisable thresholds of abuse. Therefore, CCE requires understanding the juxtaposition of legal definitions and psychological processes: recognising exploitation as a form of child abuse in law while also attending to the relational, emotional, and developmental dynamics through which harm is produced and sustained. This book builds on these debates by offering a process-oriented framework that centres early-stage dynamics of exploitation, with particular attention to children's lived experiences and pathways into and out of harm.

These tensions become particularly evident when comparing the legal and policy framing of CCE in the United Kingdom with approaches adopted in other countries. Although children in many jurisdictions experience similar forms of harm—such as involvement in drug distribution, gang-related activity, and organised crime—the legal categorisation and system responses differ significantly (Marshall, 2024; Maxwell et al., 2026). In England and Wales, CCE is increasingly recognised within safeguarding and youth justice policy as a form of child abuse (Home Office, 2018; Maxwell et al., 2019). National guidance explicitly states that a child may be criminally exploited even where their involvement appears consensual or where they have committed criminal offences (Home Office, 2018; Maxwell, 2024). This framing is reinforced through youth justice policy, particularly the Youth Justice Board's Child First principle, which prioritises children's welfare, development, and rights and seeks to minimise criminalisation and system entrenchment.

1.1.2 Defining child criminal exploitation

Within England and Wales, CCE is widely defined as a form of child abuse occurring when an individual or group takes advantage of an imbalance of power to coerce, control, manipulate, or deceive a child under the age of 18 into criminal activity for the benefit of others. The exploitation may involve violence or threats of violence, but it may also appear consensual or transactional. Crucially, a child may be criminally exploited even where they do not perceive themselves as a victim.

> Child Criminal Exploitation occurs where an individual or group takes advantage of an imbalance of power to coerce, control, manipulate or deceive a child or young person under the age of 18 into any criminal activity (a) in exchange for something the victim needs or wants, and/or (b) for the financial or other advantage of the perpetrator or facilitator and/or (c) through violence or the threat of violence. The victim may have been criminally exploited even if the activity appears consensual. Child Criminal Exploitation does not always involve physical contact; it can also occur through the use of technology.
>
> (HM Government, 2018, p. 48)

Although there is no single statutory definition of CCE in England and Wales (The Children's Society, 2019a, 2019b), the Home Office (2023) defines CCE as occurring where an individual or group "takes advantage of an imbalance of power to coerce, control, manipulate or deceive a child or young person under the age of 18 into any criminal activity". Notably, this definition recognises that exploitation may occur even where the child appears to consent or demonstrates agency, reflecting a growing understanding that consent is rendered meaningless within contexts of coercion, threat, and dependency.

This definition foregrounds three core elements: power imbalance, coercion or control, and benefit to the exploiter. It explicitly challenges assumptions of free choice and individual responsibility, recognising that children's involvement in criminal activity must be understood within the constraints imposed by grooming, fear, dependency, and structural vulnerability. As such, UK frameworks position CCE firmly within safeguarding and child protection systems rather than solely within criminal justice responses (The Children's Society, 2019a, 2019b).

The Youth Justice Board (YJB, 2022) further situates CCE within its Child First framework, which emphasises that children involved in harmful behaviour should be understood primarily as children with unmet needs, rather than as offenders to be punished. From this perspective, CCE is not an isolated event but a manifestation of wider structural, relational, and developmental harms, requiring responses that prioritise protection, prevention, and long-term well-being rather than criminalisation. Marshall (2023) provides a critical examination of the relationship between CCE and the child-first approach in youth justice. While CCE has been promoted as a model capable of reframing children involved in crime as victims rather than offenders, the paper demonstrates that, in practice, it often fails to reverse processes of "offenderisation". Delays and limitations within the National Referral Mechanism, combined with the use of criminal justice measures as forms of safeguarding, frequently result in children remaining embedded within the youth justice system. Furthermore, the category of "CCE victim" is inherently selective and shaped by narrow normative expectations of victimhood (Marshall, 2023). As a result, children whose experiences of exploitation do not meet these thresholds risk exclusion from support, despite significant unmet needs. The responses to criminal exploitation should be situated within a broader Child-First framework, capable of addressing the needs of all children in conflict with the law without reliance on exclusionary categories or punitive interventions (Marshall, 2023). A further challenge emerges when considering the Child First approach in the context of young people who have a history of serious violent offending (Creaney & Burns, 2025). Such concerns centre around public protection and effective support of the young person.

1.1.3 Early-stage exploitation as a psychological and social process

CCE, as currently defined Children's Commissioner for England (2019a, 2019b; Home Office, 2018), is increasingly understood as a process rather than a single event, often beginning at an early stage and developing incrementally (Harding, 2020; Robinson et al., 2019). Early involvement may appear informal or low level, such as running errands, holding items, relaying messages, or spending time in particular locations (National Crime Agency, 2025; Home Office, 2018). These activities can quickly escalate into more serious criminal behaviour, including drug supply, weapon carrying, or violence. This is particularly relevant in relation to drug trafficking, where criminal markets may exploit social and economic vulnerability, local marginalisation, and exposure to organised criminal networks, progressively drawing young people into income-generating offending and wider exploitative processes (Bussu et al., 2024).

Early-stage exploitation is frequently relational and emotionally embedded (Firmin, 2017; Barnardo's, 2021). Children may perceive exploitative relationships as protective or mutually beneficial, particularly where alternative sources of support, identity, or belonging are limited (Firmin, 2017). This contributes to delayed disclosure and resistance to professional concern, making early exploitation difficult to identify through traditional criminal justice indicators (NSPCC, 2025; Ofsted, 2018). Overall, "early-stage" does not denote a minor or preliminary form of exploitation but a processual position that precedes entrenchment and formal system recognition, in which exploitative dynamics are already active but not yet fully visible or named as such (Firmin, 2020; Harding, 2020).

Psychological research and qualitative studies consistently demonstrate that CCE rarely begins with overt force or explicit threats. Instead, early-stage exploitation typically unfolds through psychological conditioning, often referred to as psychological conditioning practices that are relational, affective, and incremental (Robinson et al., 2019). Children may initially experience involvement as voluntary, rewarding, or protective, particularly where exploitative relationships provide access to status, belonging, or material resources otherwise unavailable to them (Billingham & Irwin-Rogers, 2022). This process-based understanding resonates with social–ecological models of harm, which emphasise how individual behaviour is shaped by interactions across family, peer, school, community, and structural contexts (Bronfenbrenner, 1979; Walsh, 2023). Within such ecologies, criminal exploitation becomes embedded within everyday routines and relationships, rendering it difficult for children, and professionals, to identify harm at an early stage.

A significant conceptual advance in this direction is offered by Barlow et al. (2022), who explicitly reconceptualise CCE as an emergent and dynamic pattern arising from the relational interplay among children, motivated perpetrators, and shared environments. This systemic and process-oriented understanding aligns with established critiques of linear, risk-factor-based models of victimisation, which have highlighted the limitations of relying on static indicators detached from relational, contextual, and temporal dynamics (Desai et al., 2002; Hart et al., 2003; Finkelhor, 2008). By situating exploitation within complex and adaptive systems, this approach reinforces the view that CCE unfolds over time through patterned interactions rather than constituting a discrete criminal event (Beckett & Warrington, 2014). However, while such systemic frameworks provide a robust account of how exploitation emerges and stabilises within relational and environmental contexts, they offer more limited insight into the psychological and developmental processes through which children experience, interpret, and navigate exploitation in its early stages, an analytical gap that this book seeks to address through a process-oriented psychological framework.

1.1.4 Risk factors and vulnerabilities

The pathways into early CCE are shaped by intersecting structural, relational, and individual vulnerabilities, conceptualised in this book through Figure 1.1. Rather than operating in isolation, these factors cluster and interact, creating cumulative conditions of vulnerability that heighten children's exposure to exploitation.

In this book, risk factors are not treated as linear or predictive indicators of CCE, nor as static attributes located within individual children. Instead, they are conceptualised as contextually embedded and relational conditions that shape children's exposure, perceived options, and susceptibility to coercive relationships over time, reflecting established critiques of individualised and checklist-based approaches to risk (Finkelhor, 2008; Firmin, 2020). Risk factors do not cause exploitation in a deterministic sense; rather, they form part of the broader social, emotional, and structural environments within which exploitative processes may emerge, intensify, or recede (Desai et al., 2002; Beckett & Warrington, 2014). Accordingly, the analytical focus of this book is

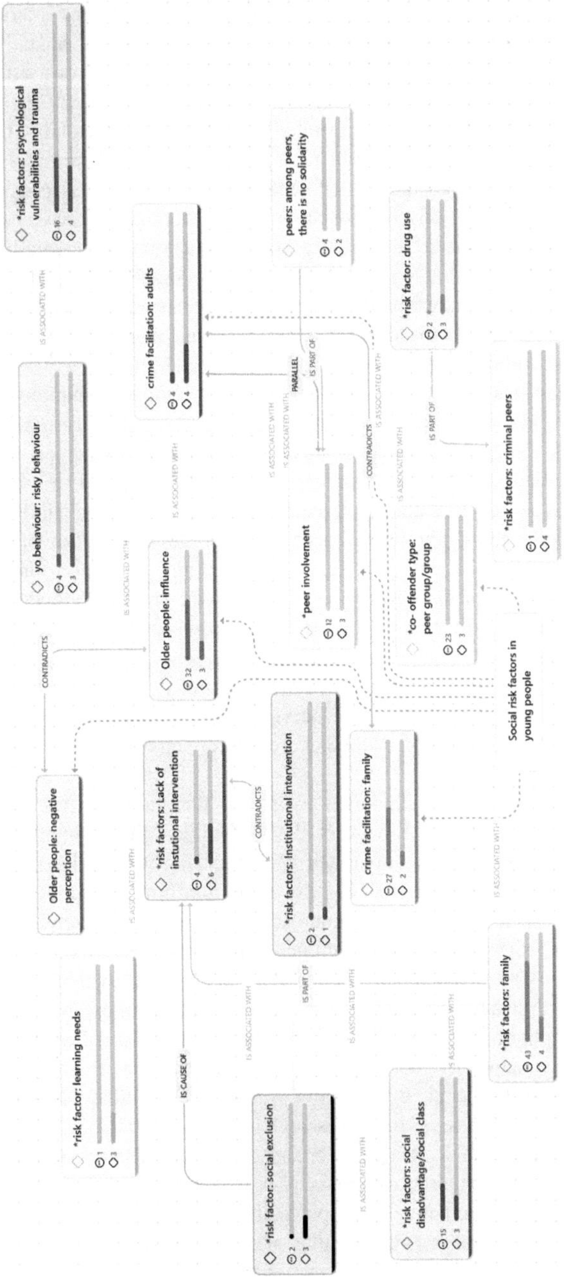

Figure 1.1 Risk factors and child criminal exploitation

not on the accumulation of risks but on how these conditions interact dynamically with psychological conditioning, power imbalances, and children's constrained agency across different stages of exploitation, consistent with process-oriented and systemic accounts of CCE (Barlow et al., 2022).

Consistent with the patterns illustrated in Figure 1.1, vulnerability to CCE emerges through the intersection of multiple risk factors rather than isolated deficits. Research across the United Kingdom and Ireland has consistently highlighted the role of poverty, educational exclusion, care experience, family adversity, and exposure to violence in shaping children's susceptibility to exploitation (The Children's Society, 2019a, 2019b; Andell & Pitts, 2017, 2023; Walsh, 2023). These vulnerabilities are not arbitrary but are concentrated within contexts that are characterised by social and economic marginalisation.

Key vulnerabilities identified within Figure 1.1 include (1) structural disadvantages, such as poverty, housing insecurity, and neighbourhood marginalisation, and a lack of institutional support; (2) exclusion from educational access, alternative social groups, opportunities, and support services (including a lack of institutional intervention); (3) family and relational adversity, such as domestic abuse, parental substance misuse, mental ill health, or care experience; (4) family and peer facilitation of criminal involvement, such as deviant social networks, social learning, and exposure to increased vulnerability through family criminal involvement; and (5) individual-level factors, including prior trauma, unmet emotional needs, low self-esteem, or neurodiversity.

Importantly, these factors should not be interpreted as causal explanations for exploitation, nor as indicators of individual deficit. Instead, they constitute conditions of heightened exposure that are actively targeted and manipulated by exploiters.

These considerations, supported by recent literature reviews in youth justice (Day et al., 2023; Malvaso et al., 2024), highlight the importance of adopting a trauma-informed approach when working with children affected by criminal exploitation. In this context, trauma-informed practice refers to approaches that recognise how trauma, coercion, fear, and chronic exposure to harm may shape children's emotions, behaviours, trust, disclosure, and engagement with professionals. Rather than interpreting avoidance, hostility, emotional detachment, or continued involvement with exploiters as wilful non-compliance, trauma-informed approaches understand these responses as potentially shaped by "survival strategies", dependency, shame, and constrained choice (Day et al., 2023; Malvaso et al., 2024; Office for Health Improvement and Disparities, 2022; Research in Practice, 2020).

As Densley (2013) demonstrates, organised criminal networks strategically identify and recruit children whose social positioning limits access to protection, legitimacy, or alternative developmental pathways. From this perspective, CCE is best understood as a manifestation of structural inequality and relational harm, rather than through individual-level explanations.

Taken together, the vulnerabilities mapped in Figure 1.1 create cumulative and reinforcing conditions through which exploitation becomes both possible and sustainable. Risk factors should therefore be understood not as predictors of offending behaviour but as markers of heightened exposure to harm within unequal social contexts. This conceptualisation underpins the analyses that follow, which draw on empirical interview data to illustrate how these vulnerabilities are experienced, negotiated, and exploited in the early stages of CCE.

Figure 1.1 demonstrates that vulnerabilities do not exist in a simple or linear relationship with one another. Social exclusion is closely tied to social disadvantage and may be associated with diminished institutional intervention, a factor that is also associated with heightened familial risk. Social risks encompass familial criminal involvement, the influence of older individuals, adult facilitation of crime, peer involvement, and peer co-offending behaviours. A negative perception of adult criminals may act as a protective factor for the influence of older people from outside of the family. Family crime facilitation contradicts non-familial adult crime involvement, as contact with a non-family adult constitutes a distinct separation and represents a different source and type of exploitation, even where a child has experienced familial criminal justice involvement. In the network, risky behaviours, frequently sensation-seeking and/or income-generating in nature, were associated with psychological trauma and substance use, factors that were embedded within criminal peer networks.

1.2 Psychological framework

This section presents the empirical findings from the study to provide a framework to explain how CCE emerges and is sustained through processes of coercion, control, and constrained choice. Rather than occurring as a clearly identifiable moment, exploitation develops gradually through family learning, everyday interactions, external relationships, and opportunities that may initially be perceived by children as normal, beneficial, or even desirable. Across the data, coercion rarely appeared as immediate or overt force. Instead, it operated through subtle, relational, and cumulative mechanisms, including influence, expectation, normalisation, and the gradual shaping of behaviour over time (Atkinson-Sheppard et al., 2025). Children's early involvement in offending was often framed within contexts of learning, belonging, and opportunity, where participation appeared voluntary, even as it became increasingly structured and controlled.

Control, in this context, was exercised not only through threats or violence but also through dependency, trust, and the regulation of everyday practices. Relationships with older peers, family members, or adult offenders played a central role in shaping children's actions, often blurring the boundaries among guidance, mentorship, and exploitation. As these relationships developed, children's perceived autonomy narrowed, even where no explicit coercion was immediately visible. The concept of constrained choice is therefore critical to interpreting these findings. While children may appear agentic, their decisions are made within contexts normalised by unequal power relations, limited alternatives, and, in many cases, implicit or explicit threats (Atkinson-Sheppard et al., 2025; Maxwell, 2026). What emerges from these data is not a simple transition from choice to coercion but a gradual reconfiguration of choice itself. The findings presented in this section illustrate how coercion and control are embedded within everyday social interactions and become normalised over time, shaping pathways into deeper forms of exploitation. This is reflected in Figure 1.2, and the associated quotations are presented in Table 1.1, which together capture the relational and processual nature of early-stage CCE.

A defining feature of CCE, particularly in its early stages, is the presence of coercive control, even in the absence of overt physical violence. As illustrated

Table 1.1 Child criminal exploitation and coercion (Figure 1.2)

Quote	*Participant A (Adult) Y (Young)*	*Theme*	*Quotation*
1.1	A23	Learning	[I was] about 8 or 9, it was a little bit of erm . . . basically you know when you're younger and that and you see the old'ens . . . the old'ens doing something like weird . . . you're thinking erm, "well I'll have a go, innit". You know they're doing this; I'll have a go, they might teach me summat.
1.2	A21	Role model	I was getting advice from somebody who was like, you know, er he's dead now but he was a well-known figure at the time. And er, yeah it was . . . yeah.
1.3	Y6	Exploitation	[It was] a bit of both. It was like, they was basically cribbing us to do their bidding, cause if we, basically what my dad turned around to me a few months ago and we was speaking about it, and he said, "Do you realise now"—they were using kids—they was using kids because no copper's going to suspect a 13-year-old, a 14-year-old to be carrying round a knife or a bleeding—stuff on them to sell- and when I heard that I just thought in my head, "Oh my god, that's true", cause police won't look at us, we was just little kids who were dressed in tracksuits and that.
1.4	Y6	Exploitation	So I was more or less—it was just like "wow—that's actually the most realest think I've heard ever," cause we didn't see it as that—we didn't see it as, like, "Oh we're kids, so we're being used by the elders to do stuff cause no one's going to suspect it". We just thought it was respect. We're part of the family here, aren't we. No, we was basically bait.

(*Continued*)

Table 1.1 (Continued)

Quote	*Participant A (Adult) Y (Young)*	*Theme*	*Quotation*
1.5	Y1	Process	It was mainly—I started off, like selling weed for—obviously I don't want to mention names, but quite, you know, quite a high—big family in S[Town], like, and I was selling it for them, and I was selling the weed and, you know, they handed me a bit of coke and said, you know, try selling that.
1.6	Y1	Training	In the house, yeah. It's like a bando, isn't it, like a trap house, isn't it, so- and then from there, you know, you just do your thing, really, isn't it, like, they'll stay with me for, like, a couple of days showing me the ropes and that, and then they'll tell me when to whip and when to bag up and when to cool it and all that.
1.7	Y17	Trauma	It's not nice, you see things you don't wanna see, but just makes you the person who you are, basically, you've just got to get a grip of it, grow up.
1.8	Y17	Trapped	A lot goes through you head at the moment, it's just want to get it over and done with cause you get yourself stuck into a situation that you can only get out of, basically, but it's hard to get out of, you've got no one to tell, you don't want to tell anyone basically, you can't tell your much cause what your mum gonna do, you know she can't.
1.9	Y9	Trauma Trapped	I had to go out and do what I had to do . . . regardless. Didn't want to do it, but I had to.

in Figure 1.2 (see also quotations in Table 1.1), coercion emerges not as a single act but as a cumulative and relational process, embedded within everyday interactions, expectations, and power asymmetries between children and those exploiting them. Participant A23 (quote 1.1) referenced early exposure to and mimicking of criminal role models as a child, without fully understanding the consequences of the behaviour. Another adult interviewee (A21, quote 1.2) had approached a known organised criminal network because he saw the adults as role models and a means of making money that would otherwise be unavailable. The process of criminal adults exploiting children to avoid police detection was described by participant Y6 (quotes 1.3 and 1.4), who was 16 years old at the time of the interview and who, by his own disclosure, did not fully understand the risk that criminal exploitation posed until after he had escaped the abuse. Y1 (quotes 1.5 and 1.6) described a process in which his abilities were progressively tested, alongside an escalation from local drug distribution to drug production and, ultimately, the transportation of drugs to another region of the country, occurring within the context of human trafficking victimisation. Participants Y17 (quotes 1.7 and 1.8) and Y9 (quote 1.9) described the associated trauma and feelings of entrapment.

The networked patterns of criminal exploitation and coercion highlight how exploitative dynamics are sustained through a combination of intimidation, normalisation, and gradual erosion of autonomy rather than immediate force. Drawing on insights from research on coercive relationships and organised crime, scholars have highlighted how debt bondage, intimidation, isolation, and emotional manipulation function to restrict children's perceived choices over time (Maxwell et al., 2019; Walsh, 2023). These dynamics help explain why children may continue engaging in criminal activity despite experiencing fear, harm, or ambivalence.

Children who are criminally exploited by organised crime groups may experience substantial barriers to accepting support or exiting exploitative contexts such as county lines (Marshall, 2024; Youth Justice Board, 2022). These barriers include deliberate social isolation from family, peers, and institutions; fear of serious harm or reprisals against themselves or loved ones; feelings of shame, denial, or emotional attachment arising from manipulative or violent exploitation; and the enduring impact of trauma, which can undermine self-confidence and agency. Practical constraints, including coercive control over basic resources, debt bondage, and structural poverty, further entrench dependency on exploiters and significantly limit children's perceived and actual capacity to disengage (County Lines Pathfinder, 2022).

The concept of constrained choice is therefore central to understanding early-stage exploitation. While children may appear agentic, their decisions are made within contexts characterised by limited alternatives, real or perceived threats, and profound power imbalances (Hesketh & Robinson, 2019; Maruna & Mann, 2019). Recognising coercion as relational, cumulative, and embedded within everyday practices is essential to avoiding responses that inadvertently criminalise victimisation and to developing interventions that address the structural and relational conditions sustaining exploitation (Colvin, 2000).

1.2.1 A process-oriented framework for early criminal exploitation

Prior research has indicated that some incarcerated adults can identify an older criminal "mentor" who influenced their involvement in crime (Morselli et al., 2006). To understand this pathway of exploitation, the offences reported by our participants were dichotomously coded alongside the age of the co-offender and their relationship to the participant. Drawing on our interviews, Figure 1.3 illustrates this phenomenon through a three-dimensional smallest space analysis (SSA) with a coefficient of alienation of .07144, showing a good fit. The analysis identified four discrete regions, supporting the adoption of a broader definition of CCE. The process starts within the family through exposure to violence and training in

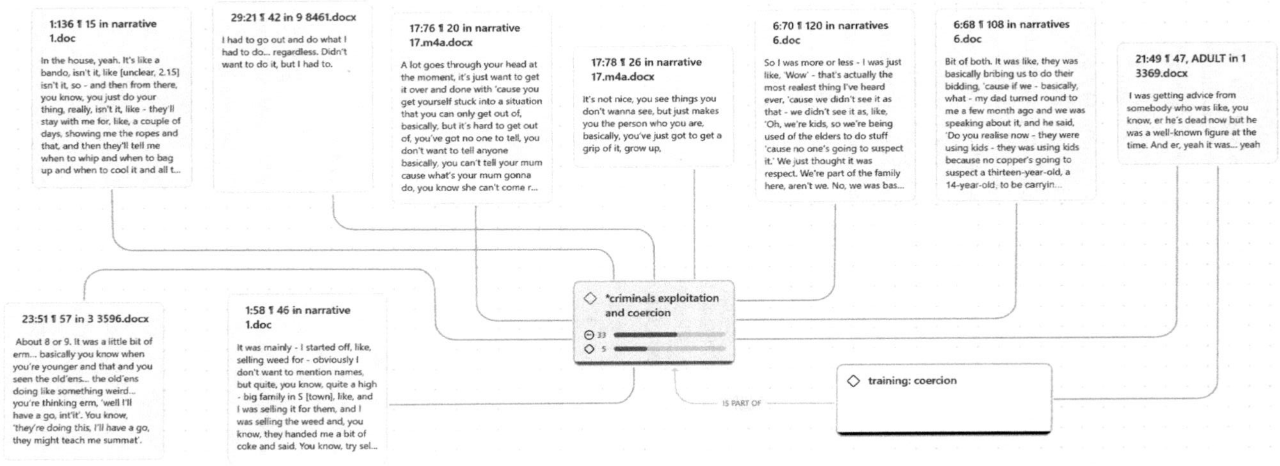

Figure 1.2 Child criminal exploitation and coercion

income-generating offending, such as theft (Figure 1.3, region and stage 1), before moving to peer-group sensory offending, such as joyriding in a stolen vehicle (TOMV), and expressive offending, such as assault (region and stage 2). Some offences (burglary and theft of a motor vehicle) appear close to peer co-offenders and adults in their 20s. The narratives indicated that this was because theft of a motor vehicle sometimes occurred under the supervision of a young adult who may be unrelated to, or associated with, one of the young people in the group, and in these cases, the car was stolen for the purposes of another offence. Interviewees described an older person instructing them and a group of peers in domestic burglary, which explains why this offence appears close to both peers and young adult co-offenders on the plot. For this reason, exploitation by a young adult is associated with enhanced offending skills and crimes that serve a secondary purpose, such as trespass, arson, and carjacking (region and stage 3). This stage is related to drug dealing and gang/group fighting under the instruction of a street-level criminal group with some elders in their 20s. The final stage (region 4) of CCE represents involvement with older, organised criminal groups and an increased exposure to violence. Robbery and weapon carrying appear in this central part of the plot, suggesting that the previous stages are potential pathways to a traditional definition of CCE. This publication adopts a broader definition of CCE, encompassing early psychological conditioning and social learning experiences that can increase young people's vulnerability to exploitation and control by organised criminal groups, as recognised in current UK policy.

Figure 1.3 Smallest space analysis showing the relationship among the age of co-offender, their relationships, and the type of criminal exploitation.

The adult interviewees were asked to complete an expanded adverse childhood experiences (ACEs) questionnaire based on the original CDC-Kaiser measure (Felitti et al., 1998), supplemented with additional indicators commonly used in expanded and urban ACEs studies to capture family instability, system involvement, and severe loss (see Cronholm et al., 2015). The mean score for the 14 valid items was 6.36, with a standard deviation of 3.64 and a range between 1 and 13. The scale had Cronbach's alpha of .84, showing good internal consistency and strong reliability for our sample. The most reported adversities were family violence/abuse and divorce (Table 1.2), and a further 63.6% of the sample witnessed their mother being abused and felt unloved or unsupported. Just under half of the sample lived with a substance user as a child, and over half shared a home with someone suffering from mental illness. Food and home insecurities were cited by 27.3% of the sample, and 18.2% of the adults who were interviewed reported having been sexually assaulted during their youth.

In addition to this questionnaire, we also asked participants at what age they had first broken the law. The adults had a mean age of 12.73 with a standard deviation of 2.97 and a range between 7 and 18 years of age. Because they were no longer involved in the social offending networks of their youth, this sample was less guarded and more able to articulate early risks within their family and peer contexts compared to the adolescent sample. Of the adult sample, 63.6% had experienced anxiety and/or depression, and 18.2% suffered from Post-Traumatic Stress Disorder (PTSD) as a child. Although 27.3% reported never using drugs, these tended to be older participants who were children when drugs were not widely available. Others reported first using drugs between the ages of 10 and 13 years (27.3%), between the ages of 14 and 15 years (18.2%), after the age of 15 (18.2%), and as an adult (9.1%). Those who had used illegal substances reported cannabis (72.7%), amphetamines (27.3%), and cocaine (18.2%). Nearly half of the sample (45.5%) used drugs with same-age friends and/or older friends, and 36.4% reported using drugs as a child alone. When asked about solo drug use, the interviewees said that they were "self-medicating" for trauma. Their ACEs scores and narrative revealed vulnerability and trauma from a young age, particularly regarding exposure to violence as a victim and witness (Table 1.2).

1.2.2 Early identification and intervention of criminal child exploitation

Early identification of the criminal exploitation of children depends on a shared local definition, cross-sector training and awareness, effective information-sharing between partners, and trust-based engagement with children, enabling timely, child-centred intervention before harm escalates. Early identification of exploitation should therefore trigger preventive, diversionary, and supportive interventions, rather than deeper system contact (Action for Children & CYCJ, 2025). Aligned with this approach, the Youth Justice Board's Child First framework provides a critical lens for responding to early-stage CCE.

Table 1.2 Extended adverse childhood experiences for the adult sample

Item	%
1. Did a parent or other adult in the household often swear at you, insult you, put you down, or humiliate you? Or act in a way that made you afraid that you might be physically hurt?	72.7
2. Did a parent or other adult in the household often or very often push, grab, slap, or throw something at you? Or ever hit you so hard that you had marks or were injured	81.8
3. Did an adult or person at least 5 years older than you ever touch or fondle you, or have you touch their body in a similar way? Or attempt to have, or actually have, oral or anal sex with you?	18.2
4. Did you often or very often feel that no one in your family loved you or thought you were special? Or did your family not look out for each other, feel close to each other, or support each other?	63.6
5. Did you often or very often feel that you didn't have enough to eat, had to wear dirty clothes, and had no one to protect you? Or were your parents too drunk or high to take care of you or take you to the doctor if you needed it?	27.3
6. Were your parents ever separated or divorced?	72.2
7. Was your mother or stepmother often pushed, grabbed, slapped, thrown at, kicked, bitten, hit with a fist or something hard, threatened with a knife or gun, or repeatedly hit over at least a few minutes?	63.6
8. Did you live with anyone who was a problem drinker or alcoholic, or who used street drugs?	45.5
9. Was any household member depressed or mentally ill?	54.6
10. Did a household member ever go to prison before you turned 17?	36.4
11. Did you ever live in a foster home before you turned 17?	0
12. Were you raised at times in your life in a single-parent family before you turned age 17?	54.5
13. Were you ever homeless before you turned 17?	27.3
14. Was any family member other than yourself physically disabled in a major way before 17?	0
15. Was your mother or father younger than 18 when you were conceived?	9.1
16. Did a household member ever attempt suicide before you turned age 17?	0
17. Did one of your biological parents or siblings commit suicide before you turned 17?	0
18. Did any of your biological parents or siblings die before you turned age 17?	0

By prioritising children's rights, well-being, and positive identity development, Child First challenges punitive responses that risk entrenching harm and criminalisation (YJB, 2022; Haines & Case, 2015).

From this perspective, early-stage CCE represents a crucial window for intervention, where coordinated multi-agency responses can disrupt exploitation trajectories before they become entrenched. Recognising early warning signs, understanding risk factors as mapped in Figure 1.1, and listening to children's lived experiences are central to this approach and underpin the empirical analyses developed in the chapters that follow (Marshall, 2023). Effective safeguarding requires early, context-sensitive identification of vulnerability indicators, recognising that these may be ambiguous, contested, or denied by children themselves, and a proactive, Child-First response that prioritises protection over criminalisation to prevent escalation along the exploitation continuum. We will argue, based on the interviews for this study, that criminal exploitation of children can occur before any involvement with organised criminal groups, at a much younger age, and for a wider variety of income-generating offences.

1.3 Implications for practice

Overall, this chapter has conceptualised CCE as a processual, relational, and developmentally embedded form of harm, with particular attention to its early stages according to the established ties to organised crime and modern slavery but also regarding earlier exploitation by family members and peer associates. Drawing on both existing scholarship (Barlow et al., 2022; Firmin, 2017, 2020; Harding, 2020; Robinson et al., 2019) and the empirical evidence informing this book, vulnerability, risk, and agency have been reframed within a nondeterministic and systemic framework that foregrounds how exploitation is learnt, normalised, and sustained over time.

This conceptual framing also carries important implications for practice. Understanding CCE as an early-stage, processual, and relational form of harm requires practitioners to move beyond event-focused thresholds and offence-led responses and to attend instead to patterns of involvement, relational dynamics, and gradual shifts in children's agency over time (Barlow et al., 2022). Early indicators of exploitation may therefore be subtle, normalised, and embedded within everyday routines, calling for professional curiosity, longitudinal engagement, and multi-agency responses that prioritise interpretation and relationship-building over premature categorisation or attribution of culpability (Maxwell et al., 2026).

Child vulnerability to exploitation may be identifiable within official records at an earlier stage than previously acknowledged (Ashton, 2023). Greater attention to the presence of older co-offenders at the time of a child's arrest for income–generating offences, including theft, may offer an opportunity to protect children from ongoing exploitation by criminal adults outside their familial or peer networks. The chapters that follow build on this conceptual foundation by examining the organisation of exploitation, the psychological processes of entrenchment, and the conditions under which disengagement and desistance may become possible, as evidenced within the research data. In this way, children are considered victims/survivors and are distinguished from the adult perpetrators who exploit them.

References

Action for Children, & Children and Young People's Centre for Justice (CYCJ). (2025). *Scotland's framework for practice: The criminal exploitation of children.* Action for Children. https://www.cycj.org.uk/resource/criminal-exploitation-of-children-cec-framework-for-practice/

Andell, P., & Pitts, J. (Eds.). (2023). *The Palgrave handbook of youth gangs in the UK*. Palgrave Macmillan.

Andell, P., & Pitts, J. (2017). *Preventing the violent and sexual victimisation of vulnerable gang involved and gang affected children and young people in Ipswich: A report for Suffolk County Council*. University of Suffolk. https://www.drugsandalcohol.ie/27822/1/Preventing_the_violent_and_sexual_victimisation_of_vulnerable_gang_involved.pdf

Ashton, S. A. (2023). *Pathways to adolescent male violent offending*. Routledge.

Atkinson-Sheppard, S., Dando, C., Ormerod, T., & Robinson, B. (2025). Coercion and crime: Convergences, divergences and 'county lines'. *Criminology & Criminal Justice, 25*(3), 927–949. https://doi.org/10.1177/17488958231153981

Barlow, C., Kidd, A., Green, S. T., & Darby, B. (2022). Circles of analysis: A systemic model of child criminal exploitation. *Journal of Children's Services, 17*(3), 158–174. https://doi.org/10.1108/JCS-04-2021-0016

Barnardo's. (2021). *Exploited and criminalised: What can the police, crime, sentencing and courts bill do to ensure that children who are criminally exploited receive the care and support they need?* Barnardo's. https://www.barnardos.org.uk/research/exploited-and-criminalised

Beckett, H., & Warrington, C. (2014). *Suffering in silence: Children and unreported crime*. University of Bedfordshire.

Billingham, L., & Irwin-Rogers, K. (2022). *Against youth violence: A social harm perspective*. Bristol University Press. https://doi.org/10.51952/9781529214086

Bronfenbrenner, U. (1979). *The ecology of human development: Experiments by nature and design*. Harvard University Press.

Bussu, A., Dettori, D. G., Ladu, M. G., & Pulina, M. (2024). Illegal drugs and socio-economic changes in a new pivotal region: A court judgements perspective. *Humanities and Social Sciences Communications, 11*, Article 1527. https://doi.org/10.1057/s41599-024-03889-3

Children's Commissioner for England. (2019a). *Keeping kids safe: Improving safeguarding responses to gang violence and criminal exploitation*. London: Children's Commissioner for England. https://assets.childrenscommissioner.gov.uk/wpuploads/2019/02/CCO-Gangs.pdf

Children's Commissioner for England (2019b). *The characteristics of gang-associated children and young people*. London: Children's Commissioner for England. https://assets.childrenscommissioner.gov.uk/wpuploads/2019/02/CCO-Characteristics-of-Gang-Associated-Children-and-Young-People1.1.pdf

The Children's Society. (2019a). *Criminal exploitation and county lines: Practitioner briefing*. The Children's Society.

The Children's Society. (2019b). *Counting lives: Responding to children who are criminally exploited*. London. https://www.childrenssociety.org.uk/sites/default/files/counting-lives-re-port.pdf (accessed 30 December 2025).

Colvin, M. (2000). *Crime and coercion: An integrated theory of chronic criminality*. St. Martin's Press.

County Lines Pathfinder, Suffolk Youth Justice Service. (2022). *Child criminal exploitation: Safe and effective exit* (Briefing paper). Youth Justice Board.

Creaney, S., & Burns, S. (2025). The Achilles heel of child first: High-risk panels in youth justice service policy and practice. *Probation Journal*. Advance online publication. https://doi.org/10.1177/02645505251353719

Cronholm, P. F., Forke, C. M., Wade, R., Bair-Merritt, M. H., Davis, M., Harkins-Schwarz, M., Pachter, L. M., & Fein, J. A. (2015). Adverse childhood

experiences: Expanding the concept of adversity. *American Journal of Preventive Medicine*, *49*(3), 354–361. https://doi.org/10.1016/j.amepre.2015.02.001
Dando, C. J., Ormerod, T. C., & Atkinson-Sheppard, S. (2023). Parental experiences of the impact of grooming and criminal exploitation of children for county lines drug trafficking. *Journal of Public Health*, *45*(2), e346–e354. https://doi.org/10.1093/pubmed/fdac112
Day, A., Malvaso, C., Butcher, L., O'Connor, J., & MacLachlan, K. (2023). Coproducing trauma-informed youth justice in Australia? *Safer Communities*, *22*(2), 106–120. https://doi.org/10.1108/SC-08-2022-0030
Densley, J. A. (2013). *How gangs work: An ethnography of youth violence*. Palgrave Macmillan.
Desai, S., Arias, I., Thompson, M. P., & Basile, K. C. (2002). Childhood victimisation and subsequent adult revictimisation assessed in a nationally representative sample of women and men. *Violence and Victims*, *17*(6), 639–653. https://doi.org/10.1891/vivi.17.6.639.33725
Felitti, V. J., Anda, R. F., Nordenberg, D., Williamson, D. F., Spitz, A. M., Edwards, V., Koss, M. P., & Marks, J. S. (1998). Relationship of childhood abuse and household dysfunction to many of the leading causes of death in adults: The Adverse Childhood Experiences (ACE) study. *American Journal of Preventive Medicine*, *14*(4), 245–258. https://doi.org/10.1016/S0749-3797(98)00017-8
Finkelhor, D. (2008). *Childhood victimization: Violence, crime, and abuse in the lives of young people*. Oxford University Press.
Firmin, C. (2017). *Contextual safeguarding: An overview of the operational, strategic and conceptual framework*. London: University of Bedfordshire.
Firmin, C. (2020). *Contextual safeguarding and child protection: Rewriting the rules*. Routledge.
Haines, K., & Case, S. (2015). *Positive youth justice: Children first, offenders second*. Policy Press.
Harding, S. (2020). *County lines: Exploitation and drug dealing among urban street gangs*. Bristol University Press.
Hart, S. D., Kropp, P. R., Laws, D. R., Klaver, J., Logan, C., & Watt, K. A. (2003). *The risk for sexual violence protocol (RSVP): Structured professional guidelines for assessing risk of sexual violence*. Mental Health, Law, and Policy Institute, Simon Fraser University.
Hesketh, R. F., & Robinson, G. (2019). Grafting: "The boyz" just doing business? Deviant entrepreneurship in street gangs. *Safer Communities*, *18*(2), 54–63. https://doi.org/10.1108/SC-05-2019-0016
HM Government. (2018). *Serious violence strategy*. https://www.gov.uk/government/publications/serious-violence-strategy
Home Office. (2018). *Criminal exploitation of children and vulnerable adults: County lines*. UK Government. https://www.gov.uk/government/publications/criminal-exploitation-of-children-and-vulnerable-adults-county-lines/criminal-exploitation-of-children-and-vulnerable-adults-county-lines
Home Office. (2023). *Criminal exploitation of children and vulnerable adults: County lines*. https://www.gov.uk/government/publications/criminal-exploitation-of-children-and-vulnerable-adults-county-lines/criminal-exploitation-of-children-and-vulnerable-adults-county-lines
Malvaso, C. G., Day, A., & Boyd, C. M. (2024). The outcomes of trauma-informed practice in youth justice: An umbrella review. *Journal of Child & Adolescent Trauma*, *17*, 939–955. https://doi.org/10.1007/s40653-024-00634-5

Marshall, H. (2023). Victims first? Examining the place of 'child criminal exploitation' within 'child first' youth justice. *Children & Society*, *37*(4), 1156–1170. https://doi.org/10.1111/chso.12696

Marshall, H. (2024). Child criminal exploitation and the interactional emergence of victim status. *The British Journal of Criminology*, *64*(5), 1011–1027. https://doi.org/10.1093/bjc/azae008

Maruna, S., & Mann, R. (2019). Reconciling "desistance" and "what works". *Academic Insights*, *1*, 3–10.

Maxwell, N. (2024). *Child criminal exploitation* (**Academic Insights 2024/04**). HM Inspectorate of Probation.

Maxwell, N., Khurana, K., & Cserző, D. (2026). 'They're not seeing young people as victims': Professional perspectives on policy and practice for criminally exploited children in Wales. *Youth Justice*, 14732254261428267.

Maxwell, N., Wallace, C., Cummings, A., Bayfield, H., & Morgan, H. (2019). *A systematic map and synthesis review of child criminal exploitation*. Cardiff University. https://orca.cardiff.ac.uk/id/eprint/131950/

Morselli, C., Tremblay, P., & McCarthy, B. (2006). Mentors and criminal achievement. *Criminology*, *44*(1), 17–43. https://doi.org/10.1111/j.1745-9125.2006.00041.x

National Crime Agency. (2025). *County lines strategic threat risk assessment 2024–2025*. National Crime Agency. https://www.npcc.police.uk/SysSiteAssets/media/downloads/publications/publications-log/national-crime-coordination-committee/2025/county-lines-strategic-threat-risk-assessment-fy-2024-25.pdf

NSPCC. (2025). *Protecting children from child criminal exploitation*. https://learning.nspcc.org.uk/child-abuse-and-neglect/child-criminal-exploitation

Office for Health Improvement and Disparities. (2022). *Working definition of trauma-informed practice*. UK Government. https://www.gov.uk/government/publications/working-definition-of-trauma-informed-practice/working-definition-of-trauma-informed-practice

Ofsted. (2018). *Protecting children from criminal exploitation, human trafficking and modern slavery: An addendum* (Reference no. 180032). https://www.gov.uk/government/publications/protecting-children-from-criminal-exploitation-human-trafficking-and-modern-slavery-addendum

Research in Practice. (2020). *Developing and leading trauma-informed practice*. Research in Practice. https://tce.researchinpractice.org.uk/wp-content/uploads/2020/02/Developing-and-leading-trauma-informed-practice.pdf

Robinson, G., McLean, R., & Densley, J. (2019). Working county lines: Child criminal exploitation and illicit drug dealing in Glasgow and Merseyside. *International Journal of Offender Therapy and Comparative Criminology*, *63*(5), 694–711. https://doi.org/10.1177/0306624X18806742

Walsh, C. (2023). *From contextual to criminal harm: Young people's perceptions and experiences of child criminal exploitation (CCE) in Northern Ireland*. Department of Justice (Northern Ireland). https://www.drugsandalcohol.ie/38748/1/Criminal_harms_final_2_.pdf

Youth Justice Board. (2022). *Child criminal exploitation: Safe and effective exit*. County Lines Pathfinder Programme. https://yjresourcehub.uk/wp-content/uploads/media/Child_Criminal_Exploitation_Safe_and_Effective_Exit_Briefing_Paper_County_Lines_Pathfinder_2022.pdf

2 Co-offending roles, training, and progression through the ranks

2.1 Conceptual framework

This chapter explores the roles of co-offending, training within crime groups, and the progression of offenders through the criminal ranks. Co-offending refers to the act of committing a crime alongside others, with the number of offenders varying from one other individual to a larger group. However, it typically involves a temporary partnership between two or three offenders (Ashton & Bussu, 2023; Uhnoo, 2016). For some, during adolescence, this phenomenon reflects the influence of peers and social groups (Goldweber et al., 2011; Piquero et al., 2002). Co-offending can serve as a form of social interaction and a means of enhancing one's status (Calvó-Armengol & Zenou, 2004; Harding, 2014; Weerman, 2003).

For young people, such activities can provide an opportunity to learn new skills from more experienced peers (Van Mastrigt & Farrington, 2011). Gardner and Steinberg (2005) suggest that children may be more susceptible to engaging in occasional deviant behaviours due to their stage of development and tendency towards impulsive decision-making (Galvan et al., 2006; Steinberg, 2008, 2010; Thomas & McGloin, 2013). The co-offending network, whether involving the instigator, equal-role co-offenders, or followers (Ashton & Bussu, 2023), can make a crime more likely to succeed simply by capitalising on the overlapping routines and social dynamics of the group. Group-based offending can serve as a pathway into criminal behaviour for young people who would not engage in offending on their own.

A combined approach emphasises the complex interaction between an individual and their broader environment. Bronfenbrenner's *Ecological Model* (1979; Bronfenbrenner & Morris, 2006; Johns et al., 2017) focuses on the complex system of social and environmental influences that contribute to a child's development. Bronfenbrenner identified five levels of influence: the *microsystem* (in direct contact with the child, e.g., family, neighbours, and school); the *mesosystem* (the interaction of the microsystem elements); the *exosystem* (formal and informal social structures including extended family and social media); the *macrosystem* (cultural embeddedness, social norms, and broader economic and socio-political systems); and the *chronosystem* (representing

DOI: 10.4324/9781003496694-3

points of change that occur over a child's development). This final element can include expected changes that are experienced by most children (starting/changing school) and unexpected changes (parental divorce, death, etc.).

Individual experiences and characteristics are relevant to understanding how to support and protect children who encounter criminal groups and influence. ACEs and exposure to family violence are associated with youth violence (Gray et al., 2021). A lack of parental supervision, parents suffering from severe mental health issues, alcohol or drug dependency, and domestic violence can expose children to CCE by organised criminal groups (see, e.g., Longfield, 2019). For these reasons, behavioural interventions need to adopt a whole family and community approach.

Contextual safeguarding (Firmin, 2017) further extends ecological approaches by recognising that significant harm to adolescents frequently occurs beyond the family home, within peer groups, schools, neighbourhoods, and online environments. This is particularly important because digital environments may intensify children's exposure to coercive relationships, intimidation, harassment, and social control.

Research on cyberbullying and cyberstalking has shown that online victimisation can affect feelings of safety, well-being, behavioural responses, and social participation among the wider population (Bussu et al., 2023a, 2023b, 2024, 2025), highlighting the need to consider digital spaces as part of the broader ecology of vulnerability and exploitation, particularly when focusing on children (Irwin-Rogers et al., 2018).

Online environments have increasingly become spaces in which children can be conditioned, coerced, and exploited, including through social media, messaging applications, gaming platforms, and other digital communication technologies (Barnardo's, 2022; Lamphere-Englund, 2025; NSPCC, 2023; Wefers, 2024). Technology may facilitate recruitment, control, intimidation, and the normalisation of exploitative relationships beyond physical community settings, contributing to children's vulnerability to criminal and sexual exploitation.

Rather than focusing exclusively on parental capacity or intra-familial risk, contextual safeguarding conceptualises extra-familial harm as a child protection issue requiring intervention within the social contexts where abuse and exploitation occur (Firmin, 2017; Wroe, 2019). This perspective is particularly relevant to CCE and group-based offending, where children may be conditioned, manipulated, coerced, or socially rewarded through peer and adult criminal networks operating within community environments. Research on county lines and CCE demonstrates that exploitation often emerges through relational processes involving trust, status, perceived belonging, and gradual exposure to offending opportunities within social networks (Longfield, 2019; Wroe, 2019). From this perspective, co-offending cannot always be understood solely as individual delinquency or freely chosen criminal participation. Instead, involvement in group offending may reflect broader contextual vulnerabilities, including exposure to violence, deprivation, exclusion from education, ACEs, and sustained contact with exploitative peer or adult influences (Barlow et al., 2022). Contextual safeguarding, therefore, resonates with Bronfenbrenner's ecological systems theory, as both frameworks emphasise the interaction between developmental vulnerability and environmental conditions. Integrating these perspectives enables a more comprehensive understanding of how co-offending roles, criminal learning, and exploitation processes develop over time within specific social contexts.

Routine activities theory (RAT; Cohen & Felson, 1979; Clarke & Felson, 2017) is also relevant for understanding co-offending among young people. It purports that crime becomes more likely when there is a combination of motivated offenders, suitable targets (i.e., potential crime victims), and a lack of capable guardianship (such as community members, neighbours, police officers, witnesses, and even potential crime victims), which can play a pivotal role in preventing or disrupting crimes against individuals or property. However, RAT has been criticised for being overly situational and deterministic, as it focuses on immediate environmental factors while neglecting broader structural and psychological elements that shape criminal behaviour. In this regard, to understand co-offending behaviour, we believe that this framework must be integrated with other theories, such as *rational choice theory* (Clarke & Cornish, 1985; Clarke & Felson, 2017; Cornish & Clarke, 2016) and *social learning theory* (Akers, 1973; Bandura, 1977; McGloin & Thomas, 2019), to provide a more comprehensive understanding of co-offending dynamics.

Rational choice theory (RCT) (Clarke & Cornish, 1985; Clarke & Felson, 2017; Cornish & Clarke, 2016) recognises that crime can be a choice that is influenced by a child's environment and their immediate social context. For example, where the opportunity to commit a crime presents itself suddenly, the individual makes a snap decision to act. Regarding the *opportunistic* or *impulsive* crimes identified in the study, where the offenders respond to immediate situations (Ashton & Bussu, 2023), the same framework suggests that, while these crimes may appear to be unplanned, they still involve a brief cost–benefit analysis, where the perceived benefit of participating in the crime (whether through excitement, group belonging, or emotional release) outweighs any immediate risks.

In Akers' social learning theory (SLT), as discussed in McGloin and Thomas (2019), peer influence plays a pivotal role in the development of both offending and co-offending behaviour. It shapes the anticipated and actual consequences of actions within peer groups. Peers may legitimise delinquent actions, signalling that such behaviours lead to social rewards, such as status, acceptance, and friendship. This, in turn, enhances the appeal of engaging in these activities. Additionally, peers can reinforce antisocial behaviour by modelling and promoting deviant actions. When a child perceives that their friends are likely to endorse or reward delinquent behaviour, they are more inclined to partake in it, highlighting the significant influence of deviant peer networks in shaping criminal trajectories.

The interplay among RAT, RCT, and SLT is critical for understanding co-offending behaviours. Each element (what a child has learnt, the opportunity to offend, and the choice to proceed with committing a crime) represents a complex series of environmental and social influences over time.

Building on our previous empirical work on adolescent co-offending, this chapter extends the analysis of group-based offending beyond typological descriptions to examine co-offending as a dynamic social process. Our earlier findings demonstrated that co-offending roles are fluid rather than fixed, with young people shifting among instigator, follower, and equal-role positions depending on group composition, opportunity structures, and perceived status (Ashton & Bussu, 2023). This chapter develops that insight further by situating role fluidity within broader processes of criminal exploitation, training, and constrained choice, highlighting how co-offending can function simultaneously as peer socialisation, skill transmission, and a mechanism of gradual entrenchment.

2.2 Findings

The analysis of the data revealed two key, interconnected dimensions: "Crime strategies and co-offending roles" (Figure 2.1) and "Training: older and peer influence" (Figure 2.2). Each dimension, along with its subdimensions, offers valuable insights into the process of criminal engagement. These decisions are shaped by a range of influences, including status, perceived lack of choice, limited legitimate opportunities, and exposure to adult criminal coercion. Each factor contributes to the phenomenon of group offending. By drawing on multiple theoretical models and integrating previous literature, we deepen our understanding of how children navigate the transition into criminal involvement.

From a contextual safeguarding perspective, these networks can be read not only as patterns of offending but also as evidence of the social contexts in which harm, learning, coercion, and exploitation occur. Figure 2.1 (see Table 2.1 for associated quotations) illustrates how opportunity, peer influence, and role fluidity shape children's movement between impulsive and planned offending. Figure 2.2 (see Table 2.2 for associated quotations) extends this analysis by showing how peer and adult influences may operate as mechanisms of training, testing, manipulation, and gradual entrenchment. In this sense, the findings demonstrate that co-offending is not simply an individual behavioural choice but a relational and contextual process that may expose children to escalating forms of criminal exploitation.

2.2.1 Crime strategies and co-offending roles

Central to Figure 2.1 is *offender roles in co-offending*. Two opposing crime strategies were highlighted in the narratives: *impulsive* (26 quotations) and *contradictory-planned* (58 quotations). Three co-offending roles were identified in the narratives: the associated *instigator* (42 quotations) and *co-offender instigation equal role* (13 quotations), both of which contradict the *follower* (41 quotations) (see Figure 2.1).

2.2.1.1 Ability to offend opportunistically and impulsively

Two *impulsive* or *opportunistic* crimes occurred when the participants were involved in other criminal behaviour and were in contrast to *planned offending* (Figure 2.1). (We have included a selection of quotations from Table 2.1 to illustrate the network.) Y15 (quote 2.1) described an incident of riding motorbikes illegally when the group decided to burn down a vacant house. A34 (quote 2.2) explained how an argument and altercation while intoxicated resulted in the participant pulling a knife out on his assailant. Some participants were invited to join criminal activities by their friends, illustrating how delinquent peers can influence others in their circle. A22 (quote 2.3) explained how friends who had stolen a motor vehicle contacted him and asked him if he wanted to join them to go joyriding.

This aligns with RCT's (Clarke & Cornish, 1985; Clarke & Felson, 2017; Cornish & Clarke, 2016) recognition that crime can be a choice influenced by the environment and the immediate social context, where the opportunity to commit a crime presents itself suddenly, and the individual makes a snap decision to act. Regarding the *opportunistic* or *impulsive* crimes identified in the study, where the offenders respond to immediate situations, the same framework suggests that while these crimes may appear to be unplanned, they still involve a brief cost–benefit analysis, where the perceived benefit of participating in the crime (whether through excitement, group belonging, or emotional release) outweighs any immediate risks.

Some young people described being on the lookout for *opportunities* to offend either alone or as part of a pair/group. Y3 (quote 2.4) explained how, with the necessary skills to remove the lock, he had seen an opportunity to steal a motorbike while walking home one evening with a friend. This interplay between skill acquisition and impulsive decision-making underscores the importance of understanding how knowledge transfer and personal competencies can facilitate *opportunistic* crime. This is especially relevant in group contexts, where social cues and peer pressure can further encourage such behaviour and facilitate the transfer of skills (Van Mastrigt & Farrington, 2011).

Concerningly, analysis of the same datasets demonstrated that adolescent criminal involvement with older offending groups enhanced both the geographical scope and seriousness of offence level for adolescents (Ashton, 2025). This study showed that young people were exposed to higher skill levels (e.g., committing robberies) and new offending locations that were a further distance from their home base through their interactions with experienced older criminals.

McGloin and Thomas (2016) have also demonstrated that the presence of others influences decision-making regarding risky or deviant behaviour. Young people are not only more inclined to take risks but also more susceptible to peer influence when making decisions about risks and preferences (Galvan et al., 2006; Gardner & Steinberg, 2005; Steinberg, 2008, 2010; Thomas & McGloin, 2013). However, it has been noted that future research should focus on exploring "how young people use situational cues to adjust their rational decision-making before choosing to engage in deviant behavior" (McGloin & Thomas, 2016, p. 479). A study by McGloin et al. (2021) highlighted that socially interdependent decision-making may be context-dependent and stressed the importance of considering the social context when examining decisions to offend. From a contextual safeguarding perspective, these findings suggest that opportunities for offending emerge within wider peer and environmental contexts that shape adolescent decision-making, risk-taking, and exposure to harmful influences (Firmin, 2017; Wroe, 2019).

2.2.1.2 Group planning of offences

In contrast to *impulsive offending, planned offences* underscore the role of group dynamics in facilitating the planning and execution of a crime. An illustration of this is the *group decision-making process* (Y10, quote 2.5) and working as a team to implement a plan of action (A26, quote 2.6). This indicates that the group serves not only as a support network but also as a platform for sharing knowledge and strategies, which can enhance the effectiveness of criminal activities. Moreover, the role of *instigators*, who often emerge within these group settings, illustrates a hierarchical structure in the planning phase. A32 (quote 2.7), who was the *instigator* in shoplifting offences, explained how he checked the shop for cameras and then decided how to proceed. Similarly, a youth participant (Y7, quote 2.8) who often *led* a small team of peers explained how he assigned roles for the purposes of shoplifting. Such individuals demonstrate leadership abilities by assessing risk (of being caught in the act) and by determining the roles of others in the execution of the offence.

Several studies have highlighted various roles within co-offending groups, such as *instigators/recruiters*, who are often older and may include family members (Reiss, 1988; Van Mastrigt & Farrington, 2011), and joiners/followers (Moffitt, 1993; Reiss, 1988). Lopez (2008) found that adolescents involved in group property crimes tended to position themselves as central figures in the offence when describing their role. Nevertheless, adolescents can recognise distinct roles within group offending (Uhnoo, 2016). However, research demonstrates that individuals can shift their co-offending roles within a group. Specifically, the roles of *instigator* and *follower* are not fixed but can change depending on the composition of the group and the timing of the offence (Warr, 1996, 2002; Weerman, 2003). According to RAT (Clarke & Cornish, 1985; Clarke & Felson, 2017; Cornish & Clarke, 2016), young people weigh the risks and rewards of criminal activities before acting, making deliberate, calculated decisions. However, the theory also suggests that opportunity, situational factors, and individual characteristics such as impulsivity and emotional triggers can influence these decisions. Figure 2.1 demonstrates that the role of the *primary instigator* in associated *group instigation.* These two co-offending roles contradict the role of *follower* in the network.

2.2.1.3 Escalation during a criminal act

Instigators in co-offending groups demonstrated offending knowledge and took a leading role to protect or instruct their friends (Y10, quote 2.9; A28, quote 2.10). In contrast, *group instigation* was often *impulsive* (Y5, quote 2.11). The escalation of criminal behaviour during the act, especially violence, within group crimes is well documented (Piper et al., 2024). The data also suggest a tendency for criminal activities to escalate over time, reflecting a dynamic evolution in offending behaviour. As illustrated in Figure 2.1, escalation emerged as closely associated with group instigation, impulsive-to-planned offending transitions, and changing offender motivations. Initial *impulsive* acts can lead to more organised and calculated crimes, as seen in the transition from joyriding to ram-raiding described by A26 (quote 2.12). This escalation often occurs as individuals and groups obtain success in the outcomes of their initial actions, leading them to adopt more ambitious and risky strategies (Adamse, 2024). For sensation-seeking offences, this intensification can also be explained by the desire for an increased thrill or a sense of invisibility among the group (Y14, quote 2.13). Crime motivations, strategies and co-offending roles reveal a complex interplay among individual capabilities, group dynamics, and the nature of the criminal acts themselves (Ashton & Bussu, 2023). More recent quantitative evidence indicates that co-offending patterns also vary according to individual characteristics, group composition, and crime type (Bright et al., 2025). The same is true of *followers* within a group. A21 (quote 2.14) shared how he positioned himself to join older criminals (for status) to commit an organised bank cash robbery. He also referenced the excitement of taking part and the cash reward that he obtained as additional outcomes. This case study demonstrates primary and secondary motivations. The participant also revealed that after the first payout, the main motivation was financial, thus showing a change of reward from social to income. These findings further support the need for a contextual safeguarding approach by illustrating how escalation can develop within group and community contexts that normalise risk, violence, and offending behaviour over time (Firmin, 2017; Barlow et al., 2022).

Table 2.1 Crime strategies and co-offending roles in Figure 2.1

Quote #	*Participant A (Adult) Y(Young)*	*Primary*	*Secondary*	*Quotation*
2.1	Y15	Impulsive	Group instigation	Cause we were filling up the bikes and one of my mates just said, "let's fucking burn the house down", innit. So we just poured the petrol around the house and burnt it down.
2.2	A34	Impulsive	Instigator	And er, as I punched him he pulled out a flick knife and because of me drinking . . . instead of me backing off . . . I'd gone towards him and I've gone "what do you think you're doing?" . . . and he came to lunge towards me, so I picked up a piece of wood and swung it at him, at which point he's then done a runner down the road.
2.3	A22	Impulsive	Follower	Before I was just at mine, like just chilling. Then one of my mates rung me I was like, "what are you doing?" and that so I told him what I'm doing and he was like, "coming out for a bit, we've got a car", so I was like, "Yeah" and we went up to either [place 2] or [place 1] we got caught because like unmarked police, so come outside the garage and we got off driving on the wrong side of the road driving as the police, then I lost 'em and the cops was above us, so we had no way of getting out so we tried hiding and they had dogs so it was just like, "Fuck it, give up".
2.4	Y3	Impulsive	Instigator Training	Well, I don't know. I was just walking and seen the bike in the car park, and then the guy was going in the house, so—just took the locks off it, took it, started it, and then, about three in the morning, was driving, and then—you know, the ANPRs.

(*Continued*)

Table 2.1 (Continued)

Quote #	*Participant A (Adult) Y(Young)*	*Primary*	*Secondary*	*Quotation*
2.5	Y10	Planned	Group instigation	We're all, if there's a problem, we all speak about it together. We figure out if it's worth our time. We'll make a group chat of all, just us ten and we'll just proper talk about it all night and if it's actually worth it we'll just set a time to meet and we'll just settle it from there but normally it's not even worth our time because nowadays kids just messaging us, calling us saying they're going to do this and that but when we see them, they just run off so we don't even waste our time anymore.
2.6	A26	Planned	Group instigation	Taking the cars . . . we had a team of us . . . two of us would go out one night and get a car, two would go out another night. Two would wait somewhere, two would go out, get the vehicle, come and pick us up and then the next night.
2.7	A32	Planned	Instigator	You've got to plan it first if you need to do it properly. This is why people get caught. You got to plan it . . . walk in . . . know where all the cameras are straight away . . . on every single column . . . know where all the blind spots are. You've got to be clever about it. If you're not seen on camera, you're getting away with it. It's as simple as that.
2.8	Y7	Planned	Instigator	I'd tell one person to go and wait in the toilets, I'd get what I was getting, I'd go to the toilets and then as far as everyone else was seeing, me and that person don't know each other, so . . . If there were three of us, then either the second person would wait with the other person in the toilet, or he'd be grabbing stuff with the person as well and stuff.

(*Continued*)

Table 2.1 (Continued)

Quote #	*Participant A (Adult) Y(Young)*	*Primary*	*Secondary*	*Quotation*
2.9	Y10	Instigator	Planned	I had to start everything, even if my mates had problems with someone, I had to go over and do something for my mates to even figure out what they wanted to do.
2.10	A28	Instigator	Planned	So basically, I was the ringleader, so I planned it down to the t really. I did it once or twice and got away with it.
2.11	Y5	Group instigation	Impulsive	No, we all just started doing it at that same time.
2.12	A26	Group instigation	Impulsive to planned	Yeah it was fun. Just joyriding, smashing them up. And then, erm, it went from that to, er, why we doing this when we can just like put it through a shop, do you know what I mean, or supermarket.
2.13	Y14	Follower	Impulsive	It wasn't mine. It was one of my mates. So we all just did it because it was funny.
2.14	A21	Follower	Planned	So [he said] I got that there. So I just said "yeah get me on that". Sort of thing. Just to show I was willing you know . . .

2.2.2 Training: older and peer influence

2.2.2.1 Progression from positive to negative views (after-the-event realisation)

Figure 2.2 (see also Table 2.2 for associated quotes) explores the process through which young people are trained in offending skills, identifying this process as a central dimension of criminal exploitation. At the centre of the network is the relationship between processes of criminal *training and older individuals*. Participants held both *positive* (5 quotations) and *negative* (8 quotations) views of older criminals. Positive elements included increased social status, as A21 (quote 2.15) explained. He expressed a desire to be part of a group of people who had a "good name . . . [a] rep[utation]", indicating that older criminals can enhance one's social standing and provide access to financial opportunities

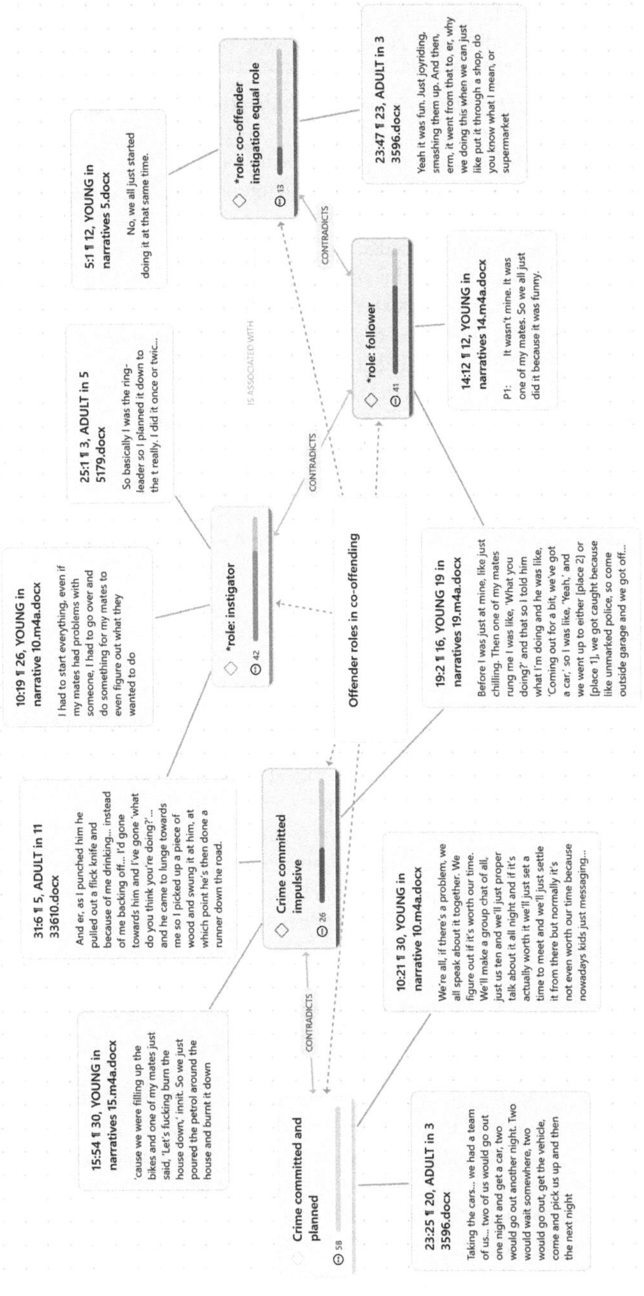

Figure 2.1 Offenders and roles in co-offending

(Y20, quote 2.16). When young people were entrenched in an organised criminal group, they also referenced positive feedback from older members. For Y1 (quote 2.17), this working relationship became what he viewed as a friendship. However, he later questioned the loyalty of his group after being arrested by the police for drug dealing.

In effect, co-offending groups provide a network of support, protection, knowledge, and specialised skills development through social learning processes between co-offenders (Andersen, 2019; McCarthy & Hagan, 2001). Conversely, many participants also acknowledge the *negative aspects* of older criminals. While younger individuals may initially feel a sense of camaraderie or mentorship, they often come to recognise the manipulative nature of these relationships. For Y20 (quote 2.18), what started out as a simple way to make money progressed to the trafficking of heroin out of the area. Many of the participants cited the influence of older criminals in their offending behaviours (32 quotations). Y10 (quote 2.19) described his realisation that he was being used to store firearms, thus also referencing enhanced exposure to violence. The influence could also be through peer friendships (A35, quote 2.20). Young people can experience both friendship and *manipulation* within these dynamics, reflecting a complex relationship where older criminals may not only provide guidance but also place younger individuals in risky situations and take advantage of them.

2.2.2.2 Training by older people

Having a *negative perception* of older individuals was identified as a protective factor, which *contrasts* with their influential role within the network, where older people were associated with the *provision of criminal training*, which was cited in 32 quotations and emerged as a critical component in the development of criminal skills and networks. The trainers consisted of *family members* (A32; Y23), *older friends* (A21; A27), and *community adult criminals* (A21). Consistent with the contextual safeguarding framework, these accounts demonstrate how criminal learning and exploitation can become embedded within peer, family, and community relationships, where influence, coercion, and belonging often intersect (Firmin, 2017; Wroe, 2019; Barlow et al., 2022).

Although some adolescent participants who had been involved with organised criminal groups recognised that they had been manipulated and coerced by elders, adult participants were more likely to reflect on this process. The influence of older figures is often seen as a rite of passage into the criminal world, with participants like A32 (quote 2.21) sharing experiences of committing crimes alongside family members. For Y23 (quote 2.22), he stole money from his mother's purse after seeing his sister do the same thing. He then progressed to stealing money from an employer when an opportunity arose. There are multiple possible relationships between the family and adolescent offending behaviours. The examples cited here illustrate direct training and criminal mentoring from older family members. Antisocial role models from within the family can normalise offending and inappropriate social responses by young people. Indirectly, family members can also influence the number of ACEs for a young person.

The SLT framework proposes that young people are more likely to engage in delinquent and criminal behaviours when they associate with peers who are already involved in such activities (Ashton & Bussu, 2023). Therefore, if young people are surrounded by peers who glorify criminal success, they are more likely to adopt similar behaviours, escalating their involvement in criminal activities.

ACEs also increase youth vulnerability. Spencer et al. (2019) found that many exploited children were living in poverty, often experiencing inadequate or unstable housing. They were also frequently exposed to multiple adverse childhood events, including physical abuse, parental substance misuse, criminal behaviour, neglect, parental mental health issues, or the absence of one or both parents. The National Crime Agency (2017) similarly identified various factors that increase children's vulnerability to criminal exploitation. These include behavioural difficulties, school exclusions, being in care, missing children, drug users, and those with physical or mental health issues. Each of these characteristics individually contributes to a child's susceptibility to exploitation, and the presence of multiple vulnerabilities significantly amplifies the risk.

Younger individuals may view their involvement as a form of bonding or friendship. However, those who had been involved with organised criminal groups and who had managed to leave were aware *of being manipulated* (Y6, quote 2.23; Y10, quote 2.19; Y20, quote 2.18). This realisation was more challenging for those who were still embedded in the process. One participant (Y15), who was embedded in an organised criminal group, did not see that he was being manipulated or used by his elders. In fact, he shared that he had been awarded "stripes" for his part in a carjacking and a subsequent sale of the stolen vehicle.

Overall, adult participants (A21, quote 2.24; A32, quote 2.21; A35, quote 2.20) tended to reflect more critically on the training process irrespective of the status of their co-offending group, suggesting that age and experience can affect perceptions of these relationships. This distinction highlights the *developmental differences* (Wikstrom et al., 2024) in how participants understand their involvement in crime, as well as the potential for growth or disillusionment as they age. As A21 became more embedded in an organised criminal group, he began to realise that the person at the top of the group was able to obtain money with no risk to himself because he instructed others to commit the armed robberies (quote 2.26).

Once trained, some participants became instigators of crimes. A28 had committed thefts with his father as a child and later initiated burglaries with his younger brother and friends (quote 2.25). A31 (quote 2.27) reflected on the process of stealing and purchasing cars, demonstrating how people of different ages could be involved in a chain of offences. The transition from *follower* to *instigator* within criminal behaviour is a multifaceted process that highlights the intricate interplay between individual motivations and broader social influences. This dynamic shift is significantly influenced by several key factors, including mentorship from older criminals, peer dynamics, and the inherent characteristics of the criminal act itself (Ashton & Bussu, 2020; Ashton, 2023). *Peer training* (2–4 quotations) could also be planned and organised. A27 (quote 2.28) described his friend's shed as a headquarters for planning. As noted previously by Y7 (quote 2.8), shoplifting in the local shop was strategic, and strict roles were enforced.

2.2.2.3 Self-training

Self-training, which contrasts with peer training in Figure 2.2, is a significant part of offending behaviours because it allows individuals to independently develop criminal skills through experience, observation, or trial and error. As offenders adapt and refine their techniques, they become more skilled and potentially have more to offer criminal groups. *Self-training* also empowers individuals, giving them a sense of ownership over their behaviour, which can deepen their involvement in crime. Additionally, this process can influence peers, as those who *self-trained* may become role models or *instigators*, spreading criminal behaviour within social groups (Hurd et al., 2011). Both youth (Y1, quote 2.29) and adult participants (A30, quote 2.30) referenced how they enhanced their criminal skills through *self-training* (three quotations). Both narratives emphasise the idea of *self-training* in criminal behaviour, where individuals become *instigators* of their own actions. They also illustrate a gradual process of deeper involvement, where social connections and repeated experiences reinforce their behaviour, making it habitual. Y1 (quote 2.31) explained how he had developed criminal networks nationally as a victim of drug trafficking. A30 (quote 2.30) described a "lightbulb" moment of building on his training by older criminals, thus illustrating the cognitive process of learning by obtaining rewards.

Understanding how young people *self-train* and develop skills through peer observation, even when applied to criminal activities, involves examining their motivations and the impact on their self-efficacy. This is crucial for reflecting on ways to foster their self-esteem and confidence in prosocial activities, thereby reducing deviance. Collaborating with young people to explore how these transferable skills can be redirected towards building a positive and prosocial identity is equally important, alongside co-producing engaging early interventions (Smithson et al., 2021).

2.2.2.4 Testing and loyalty

As illustrated throughout Figure 2.2, processes of training, testing, and loyalty appeared closely interconnected, often functioning simultaneously as mechanisms of criminal learning, social bonding, and exploitation. In Figure 2.2, *peer testing* and *testing by older criminals* appear as parallel mechanisms. However, *peer training* contradicts *testing by older criminals*, indicating a sequential process that moves from peer engagement to evaluation by older individuals. The term "tested" holds significant meaning within the context of criminal training and peer dynamics and was used in two different contexts by participants. The first was being assessed for skills or loyalty (Y1, quote 2.17). The second meaning was being challenged. In the example cited by Y6, he challenged a peer to see whether he would use the knife that he had pulled to threaten the participant. The experience of Y1, who was tested for loyalty, suggests that social acceptance within criminal groups often necessitates the demonstration of commitment, which may include engaging in dangerous or illegal activities. This notion of loyalty transcends mere allegiance to a group; it reflects a broader cultural understanding of trust and credibility within high-risk environments. In such contexts, individuals may feel compelled to participate in acts that affirm their loyalty, often under the threat of exclusion or retribution. This creates a paradox in which the very actions intended to solidify bonds may lead to greater entrenchment in criminal behaviour and, ultimately, to self-destructive patterns (Pyrooz & Densley, 2016; Vecchio & Carson, 2023).

Conversely, Y6's (quote 2.32) account of challenging a peer to use a knife exemplifies the potential for violence and conflict that can arise in these testing scenarios. This confrontation serves as a mechanism for asserting dominance and establishing one's position within the group hierarchy. *The pressure to engage in violent* acts can foster a culture of fear and aggression, compelling individuals to prove themselves in increasingly perilous ways. Such dynamics often lead to an environment where *loyalty is not only expected but also demanded*, with failure to comply resulting in severe personal consequences. Moreover, the high-stakes nature of the environment in which these young individuals operate often blurs the lines between loyalty and coercion. In criminal settings, loyalty can devolve into a survival instinct, whereby individuals engage in criminal activities not solely out of allegiance but also as a means of self-preservation. The expectations placed upon them by their peers can create a *vicious cycle*, reinforcing a culture of violence that perpetuates criminal behaviour and undermines the potential for developing prosocial behaviour. This examination of loyalty and testing within criminal contexts raises significant questions about agency and identity. It challenges the perception of individuals as mere products of their environment, suggesting instead that they navigate complex social landscapes fraught with risks and rewards.

In previous studies (see, e.g., Brezina & Azimi, 2018; Cullen, 1994; Colvin et al., 2002), peer social support typically leads to a sense of moral duty and a commitment towards the person offering support. In adolescent peer relationships, this sense of duty often takes the form of *loyalty*, which is seen as the expected response to receiving support. Alongside intimacy, adolescents consider loyalty to be a fundamental, if not defining, element of friendship (Savin-Williams & Berndt, 1990). In such friendships, loyalty means remaining reliable, trustworthy, and true to one another, with betrayal being unacceptable. As Savin-Williams and Berndt (1990) state, “First, friends must be loyal to one another; they should not ‘talk about you behind your back’” (p. 278). Loyalty holds particular significance for adolescents because these friendships often represent early attempts to establish an independent identity, making them more susceptible to fragility and insecurity (Brezina & Azimi, 2018; Warr, 2002).

Table 2.2 Training and older criminals in Figure 2.2

Quote #	*Participant A (Adult) Y(Young)*	*Primary*	*Secondary*	*Quotation*
2.15	A21	Positive	Follower Planned	Well the reason why I was in that crowd of individuals was because you know, it’s . . . I wanted to be in that group. I wanted to be . . . they had a good name . . . it was all . . . it was people . . . I won’t say looked up to but they had a rep about themselves.
2.16	Y20	Friendly Positive to negative	Follower	“Do you want to earn yourself a bit of money?” and I’m like, “Doing what?” and he’s like “Just taking something somewhere for me”, “Like what is it?” and he said “Nothing important, juz take it and I’ll give you a bit of money”. So obviously it weren’t nothing major, apparently in his eyes so he sorted out train tickets, I went up to said place which was [county] from [city] and then I got there and basically I was someone’s runner, running around [county] selling heroin and crack to people.
2.17	Y1	Positive Friendly	Training Planned Instigator to follower	I started selling a bit of, like, cocaine, like, flake, up in where I live, and one of my friends, he taught me how to, you know, whip it, and I did that, and then some people noticed it and they, you know, they said it were good. And I kind of like formed, like, a bit of a friendship with them and when I got that.

(*Continued*)

Table 2.2 (Continued)

Quote #	*Participant A (Adult) Y(Young)*	*Primary*	*Secondary*	*Quotation*
2.18	Y20	Negative	Follower	So that was, you know, like, "Yeah, you're a sound person", you don't meet many sound people. Obviously, he's not a sound person 'cause he wanted one thing and that's what he got
2.19	Y10	Older influence	Negative	They were passing me guns and knives to walk round with. I remember one time there was a 20-year-old passing me a shotgun with shotgun bullets to walk around with because the police were going to his house but because I was young at the time I thought yes I'll do it to get his respect. But now I see he was just using me to get himself out of trouble.
2.20	A35	Older influence	Negative	No. Because I . . . I was friends with the younger one so I was with him more or less day . . . most days. So, it wasn't like . . . it was, er, a random thing. Like I was . . . seen his relative a few times. I'd spoken to him. I never thought anything of it. Like I wouldn't really think that would happen.
2.21	A32	Training older	Follower	Family. Me dad used to take me out when I was younger. When we were kids he used to take me out like grafting in the middle of the night. Robbing stuff. Yeah. It were normal to me. It were normal.
2.22	Y23	Family training	Follower	Sister's idea at first, and then I'd copy her. This was, like, in year six, and then I did it. I stopped three years ago.
2.23	Y6	Family training	Follower	Kind of does, kind of does. It's like—but even when I was, like, young young, like, an actual kid, before even I was a teenager, you were seeing gang shit all about, because, like,

(*Continued*)

Table 2.2 (Continued)

Quote #	*Participant A (Adult) Y(Young)*	*Primary*	*Secondary*	*Quotation*
				I—one of my old mates—not seen him in years—used to see me when we went primary and that—we used to go his—his dad was a gangster, his dad had guns and everything like that, and you was looking at them.
2.24	A21	Training older	Follower	It was again just learned behaviours from older people, previous people. And you hear how it gets highlighted and glossy the names become because they did an armed robbery.
2.25	A28	Training older	Instigator	Because they knew, obviously they were me friends, and because I told them about the one that I did. The first one. So they wanted to get involved in it.
2.26	A21	Training older	Follower	He was well known within the area and er . . . thinking back the two of the lads who I did it with, they were trying to impress him, while I was trying to do it with these two. And, er . . . so we ended up. I jumped on that and he just said "right, you three do this and do it this way". He virtually planned it all out and said "right, don't be . . . don't be doing this, do this, go this way, do that", do you know what I mean, he had it all planned out. Er, and again thinking back at it, he obviously . . . he sat back and just made his money and didn't have to do anything. So.
2.27	A31	Training older and peers	Group	It could be [older]. Sometimes it could be a friend or sometimes it can be a friend of a friend. Like ask them do you know anyone like they want to buy a car or . . . say if you offer that car then like "right we'll buy it".

(*Continued*)

Table 2.2 (Continued)

Quote #	*Participant A (Adult) Y(Young)*	*Primary*	*Secondary*	*Quotation*
				Then it's just the same thing again. Like one person then they'll do the same thing again, and then again, and again.
2.28	A27	Peer training	Group	We just influenced each other . . . Er . . . one of the lads . . . well we all had sheds in the backyard . . . well one of them his shed was like an HQ.
2.29	Y1	Tested by adult	Follower	They'll stay with me for, like, a couple of days, showing me the ropes and that, and then they'll tell me when to whip and when to bag up and when to cool it and all that.
2.30	A30	Self-training	Instigator	And you know, once you keep on getting that same reply [clicks fingers] the lightbulb comes on [clicks fingers] and oh . . . if I go out every week and people asking me the same question . . . I might as well come out and just do what I'm doing. So, you see what I'm saying, so it's actually a process that once you understand the process you just do it.
2.31	Y1	Self-training	Instigator	And I kind of like formed, like, a bit of a friendship with them and when I got that, I got in contact with people kind of all over the country and, kind of like taking it from A to B, and that type of thing, with a few people.
2.32	Y6	Tested by peers	Instigator	So I was just fighting other people there, so—I've had people pull blades out on me and everything like that, but with me, I'm one of them people where if you do something like that, I'm like, "I'll test you"—I'll just stand there, "Okay, go on, do something", "cause most of the time they won't".

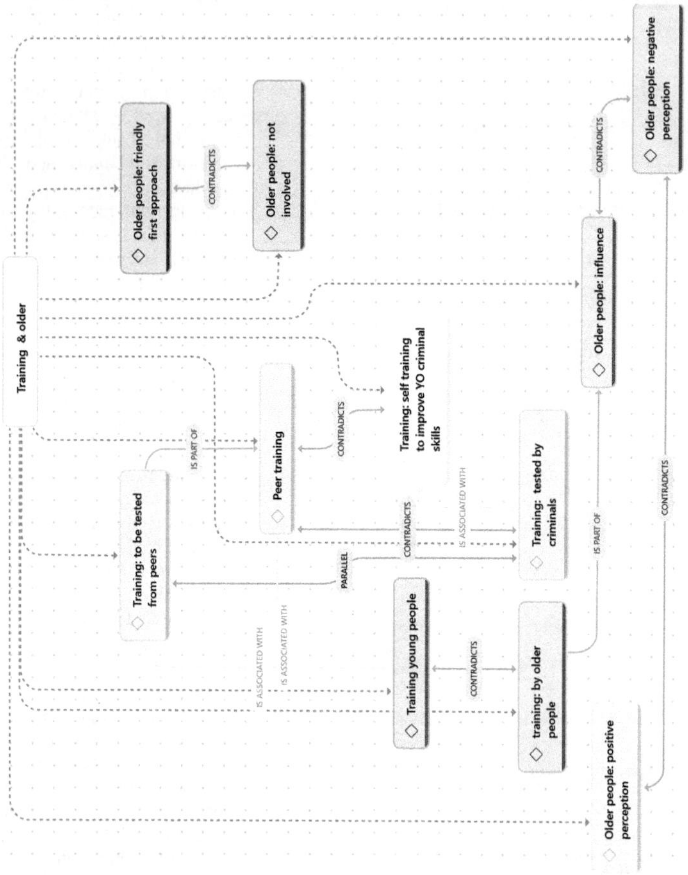

Figure 2.2 Training: older and peer influence

2.3 Implications for practice

Understanding the nuanced motivations behind youth criminal involvement is essential for developing effective early interventions and strategies. These behaviours are shaped by the complex interplay of multiple systemic levels, including individual, family, peer, school, and broader community factors. The interactions between these levels, as outlined in Bronfenbrenner's ecological systems theory (1979), highlight how changes in one domain can present new risk or protective factors.

The adults interviewed were able to critically reflect on their motivations for committing offences and recognise changes in their attitudes. Two categories emerged: (1) The transfer of reactive antisocial behaviour to the use of violence to control a situation and (2) The desire for social status gradually shifts towards financial goals and rewards. Understanding primary and secondary motivations for offending is critical for prevention. For example, prevention programmes that highlight legitimate ways to obtain status and financial rewards could be implemented in schools in socially and economically deprived areas. Preventing school disengagement and dropout may represent a crucial component of early intervention and safeguarding strategies, particularly within disadvantaged contexts where educational exclusion can increase vulnerability to exploitation, offending, and social marginalisation (Bussu & Pulina, 2020). Educational exclusion and school dropout are particularly important within this framework, as they may remove one of the most significant protective contexts in a young person's life. When children are excluded from school or become progressively disengaged from education, they may lose access not only to learning but also to stable adult relationships, routine, supervision, peer support, and opportunities for positive identity development (Lloyd, 2025). Young people also diminish their career prospects and ability to secure legitimate sources of income. In this sense, school exclusion can become a key risk factor for youth offending and criminal exploitation, particularly in disadvantaged contexts (Butler et al., 2025; Lloyd, 2025). Conversely, inclusive and supportive school environments can operate as protective spaces by strengthening belonging, resilience, social skills, and future aspirations (Bronfenbrenner, 1979; Bussu & Pulina, 2020; Bussu et al., 2022; Bussu & Burton, 2023; Youth Justice Board, 2022).

Recognising youth roles and peer group dynamics is crucial, as it can inform preventative strategies that specifically target group interactions within youth environments. Programmes for youth who are coerced or who follow as part of an offending group should focus on resistance to peer and antisocial adult influence. However, several of our participants indicated that they had acquired skills to become instigators of crime and were able to influence their siblings or peers for income-generating offences. Any responses to this next stage of criminal involvement would need to focus on changing identities from antisocial to prosocial and alternative sources of financial gain (Ashton & Bussu, 2023). Moreover, the implications of these dynamics extend beyond individual cases; they highlight the need for broader community engagement to address the factors contributing to youth deviance. By cultivating supportive environments that foster positive identities and social relationships outside of criminal networks, communities can effectively reduce the appeal and associated risks of such groups (Ashton & Bussu, 2023; Ashton & Ward, 2022; Newson et al., 2024). These experiences can play a crucial role in preventing criminal behaviour by influencing attitudes and actions. Life skills-based interventions may further strengthen this preventive approach by supporting young people's self-efficacy, emotional regulation, communication, resilience, and capacity to develop positive future-oriented identities (Bussu & Mangiarulo, 2024, 2026).

Both adolescent and adult participants identified the early stages of criminal exploitation and were able to distinguish between their initial impressions of an older criminal mentor and the reality of being involved with a criminal group and being controlled. Alerting children and young people to the processes used by criminal adults and groups to recruit/coerce them could provide critical protection at the early stages of exposure to crime.

On the basis of our findings, we propose several recommendations for practitioners, policymakers, and community organisations. Firstly, there should be a focus on developing programmes that offer mentorship, skill-building opportunities, and positive peer interactions (Bussu et al., 2024; Bussu & Mangiarulo, 2024; Creaney et al., 2026; Newson et al., 2024). Research on peer mentoring highlights the positive outcomes for young people involved in prosocial peer groups (Bussu et al., 2024; Butts et al., 2010; Humphreys & Teater, 2018). Additionally, certain peer mentoring programmes have incorporated restorative practices and changes aimed at secondary desistance (Austria & Peterson, 2017; Maruna, 2016, 2017; Humphreys & Teater, 2018).

According to our research, young people acquire criminal behaviours by observing others in their social contexts. It is important to emphasise the significance of community initiatives that create *safe spaces* for youth to interact and engage in constructive activities. Preventive measures such as early interventions should be prioritised, targeting youth before they become entrenched in cycles of criminal behaviour. This includes implementing *prosocial adult mentoring programmes* that provide positive alternatives to criminal activities (Ashton & Ward, 2022; Bussu et al., 2024).

The findings suggest that these programmes vary significantly in their impact on reducing criminal behaviour. Approaches such as mentoring and restorative justice demonstrated greater potential compared to conventional strategies centred on diversion and sanctions. A possible explanation is that informal mechanisms of social regulation within communities, such as fostering connections between service users and constructive community influences, may better promote adherence to societal norms. In contrast, formal mechanisms, including oversight by probation officers, may be less effective, potentially due to insufficient resources or skills necessary for successful implementation (Newson et al., 2024).

References

Adamse, I., Blokland, A., & Eichelsheim, V. (2024). Understanding co-offending patterns and criminal mentorship using police registry data. *Deviant Behavior*, 85–105. https://doi.org/10.1080/01639625.2024.2417271

Akers, R. L. (1973). *Deviant behavior: A social learning approach*. Wadsworth.

Andersen, S. N. (2019). Partners in crime? Post-release recidivism among solo and co-offenders in Norway. *Nordic Journal of Criminology*, *20*(2), 112–137. https://doi.org/10.1080/2578983X.2019.1606492

Ashton, S. A. (2023). *Pathways to adolescent male violent offending*. Routledge.

Ashton, S. A. (2025). A geography of early vulnerabilities and exploitation in the narratives of adolescent males in England. *Journal of Criminal Psychology*, *15*(1), 55–71. https://doi.org/10.1108/JCP-07-2024-0064

Ashton, S. A., & Bussu, A. (2020). Peer groups, street gangs and organised crime in the narratives of adolescent male offenders. *Journal of Criminal Psychology*, *10*(4), 277–292. https://doi.org/10.1108/JCP-06-2020-0020

Ashton, S. A., & Bussu, A. (2023). The social dynamics of adolescent co-offending. *Youth Justice*, *23*(3), 350–371. https://doi.org/10.1177/14732254221136044

Ashton, S.-A., & Ward, J. (2022). Bridging the gap between criminal psychology and frontline youth work: A case study in programme development and evaluation. *Assessment & Development Matters*, *14*(4), 14–17. https://doi.org/10.53841/bpsadm.2022.14.4.14

Austria, R., & Peterson, J. (2017). *Credible messenger mentoring for justice-involved youth*. The Pinkerton Foundation.

Bandura, A. (1977). *Social learning theory*. Prentice-Hall.

Barlow, C., Kidd, A., Green, S. T., & Darby, B. (2022). Circles of analysis: A systemic model of child criminal exploitation. *Journal of Children's Services*, *17*(3), 158–174. https://doi.org/10.1108/JCS-04-2021-0016

Barnardo's. (2022). *The online safety bill and child criminal exploitation*. https://www.barnardos.org.uk/sites/default/files/2022-11/Child%20Criminal%20Exploitation%20%20Knife%20Crime%20APPG%20-%20The%20Online%20Safety%20Bill%20and%20CCE%20Briefing.pdf

Brezina, T., & Azimi, A. M. (2018). Social support, loyalty to delinquent peers, and offending: An elaboration and test of the differential social support hypothesis. *Deviant Behavior*, *39*(5), 648–663. https://www.tandfonline.com/doi/full/10.1080/01639625.2017.1286190

Bright, D., Lerner, J., & Sadewo, G. R. P. (2025). Examining co-offending and re-offending across crime categories using relational hyperevent models. *Journal of Criminology*, *58*(1), 109–134. https://doi.org/10.1177/26338076241272864

Bronfenbrenner, U. (1979). *The ecology of human development: Experiments by nature and design*. Harvard University Press.

Bronfenbrenner, U., & Morris, P. A. (2006). The bioecological model of human development. In R. M. Lerner & W. Damon (Eds.), *Handbook of child psychology* (6th ed., Vol. 1, pp. 793–828). John Wiley & Sons. https://doi.org/10.1002/9780470147658.chpsy0114

Bussu, A., Ashton, S.-A., Pulina, M., & Mangiarulo, M. (2023a). An explorative qualitative study of cyberbullying and cyberstalking in a higher education community. *Crime Prevention and Community Safety*, *25*, 359–385. https://doi.org/10.1057/s41300-023-00186-0

Bussu, A., & Burton, S. (2023). Higher education peer mentoring programme to promote student community using mobile device applications. *Groupwork, 30*(2), 53–71. https://doi.org/10.1921/gpwk.v30i2.1636

Bussu, A., & Pulina, M. (2020). Exploring young people's perceptions about secondary school: Critical issues and improvements to prevent dropout risk in disadvantaged contexts. *Improving Schools*, *23*(3), 223–244. https://doi.org/10.1177/1365480220940858

Bussu, A., Creaney, S., Price, J., Burns, S., & Myles, K. (2024). "It's a sixth sense . . . I see you, you see me, and we've been there": Benefits and challenges of developing a peer mentoring scheme with young people in youth justice services. *British Journal of Community Justice*, *19*(2), 4–19. https://doi.org/10.48411/4c2h-hc54

Bussu, A., & Mangiarulo, M. (2024). Playing music together: Exploring the impact of a classical music ensemble on adolescents' life skills self-perception. *PLoS One*, *19*(7), Article e0306326. https://doi.org/10.1371/journal.pone.0306326

Bussu, A., & Mangiarulo, M. (2026). Harmony beyond the notes: Community members' perspectives on the impact of classical music ensembles on children and young people's life skills. *Journal of Community & Applied Social Psychology*, *36*(1), 1–18. https://doi.org/10.1002/casp.70221

Bussu, A., Pulina, M., Paolini, D., & Zanzuino, G. (2022). From choice to performance in secondary schools: Evidence from a disadvantaged setting in Italy. *Italian Economic Journal*, *9*(2), 529–555. https://doi.org/10.1007/s40797-021-00178-9

Bussu, A., Pulina, M., Ashton, S.-A., & Mangiarulo, M. (2023b). Exploring the impact of cyberbullying and cyberstalking on victims' behavioural changes in higher education during COVID-19: A case study. *International Journal of Law, Crime and Justice*, *75*, Article 100628. https://doi.org/10.1016/j.ijlcj.2023.100628

Bussu, A., Pulina, M., Ashton, S.-A., & Mangiarulo, M. (2025). Cyberbullying and cyberstalking in higher education: Policies and practices for supporting students and academic staff. *Social Psychology of Education*, *28*, Article 34. https://doi.org/10.1007/s11218-024-09989-x

Bussu, A., Pulina, M., Ashton, S.-A., Mangiarulo, M., & Molloy, E. (2024). Cyberbullying and cyberstalking victimisation among university students: A narrative systematic review. *International Review of Victimology*, *31*(1), 59–90. https://doi.org/10.1177/02697580241257217

Butler, N., Wilson, C., Quigg, Z., McCoy, E., Dooks, T., & Davies, A. (2025). No safe space: Impact of cumulative disadvantage of adversity in the home and exclusion from school on victimisation and offending behaviour within a justice-involved youth sample. *Public Health*, *251*, Article 106117. https://doi.org/10.1016/j.puhe.2025.106117

Butts, J. A., Bazemore, G., & Meroe, A. S. (2010). *Positive youth justice: Framing justice interventions using the concepts of positive youth development*. Coalition for Juvenile Justice.

Calvó-Armengol, A., & Zenou, Y. (2004). Social networks and crime decisions: The role of social structure in facilitating delinquent behaviour. *International Economic Review*, *45*(3), 939–958. https://doi.org/10.1111/j.0020-6598.2004.00292.x

Clarke, R. V., & Cornish, D. B. (1985). Modeling offenders' decisions: A framework for research and policy. *Crime and Justice*, *6*, 147–185. https://doi.org/10.1086/449106

Clarke, R. V., & Felson, M. (Eds.). (2017). *Routine activity and rational choice: Volume 5*. Routledge.

Cohen, L. E., & Felson, M. (1979). Social change and crime rate trends: A routine activity approach. *American Sociological Review*, *44*(4), 588–608. https://doi.org/10.2307/2094589

Colvin, M., Cullen, F. T., & Vander Ven, T. (2002). Coercion, social support, and crime: An emerging theoretical consensus. *Criminology*, *40*(1), 19–42. https://doi.org/10.1111/j.1745-9125.2002.tb00948.x

Cornish, D. B., & Clarke, R. V. (2016). The rational choice perspective. In R. Wortley & M. Townsley (Eds.), *Environmental criminology and crime analysis* (pp. 48–80). Routledge. https://www.taylorfrancis.com/books/edit/10.4324/9781315709826/environmental-criminology-crime-analysis-richard-wortley-michael-townsley

Creaney, S., Price, J., Bussu, A., Burns, S., & Myles, K. (2026). The social and educational value of peer mentoring in a youth justice context. In A. Shafi, S. Case, N. Hazel, & H. Kent (Eds.), *The Palgrave handbook on the children' in Criminal Justice Setting*. Published online in early September. https://link.springer.com/book/9783032231192#accessibility-information

Cullen, F. T. (1994). Social support as an organizing concept for criminology: Presidential address to the academy of criminal justice sciences. *Justice Quarterly*, *11*(4), 527–559. https://doi.org/10.1080/07418829400092421

Firmin, C. (2017). *Contextual safeguarding: An overview of the operational, strategic and conceptual framework*. University of Bedfordshire. https://tce.researchinpractice.org.uk/contextual-safeguarding-an-overview-of-the-operational-strategic-and-conceptual-framework/

Galvan, A., Todd, A., Hare, T. A., & Parra, C. E. (2006). Earlier development of the accumbens relative to the orbitofrontal cortex might underlie risk-taking behaviour in adolescents. *Journal of Neuroscience*, *26*(25), 6885–6892. https://doi.org/10.1523/JNEUROSCI.1062-06.2006

Gardner, M., & Steinberg, L. (2005). Peer influence on risk-taking, risk preference, and risky decision making in adolescence and adulthood: An experimental study. *Developmental Psychology*, *41*(4), 625–635. https://doi.org/10.1037/0012-1649.41.4.625

Goldweber, A., Dmitrieva, J., Cauffman, E., Piquero, A. R., & Steinberg, L. (2011). The development of criminal style in adolescence and young adulthood: Separating the lemmings from the loners. *Journal of Youth and Adolescence*, *40*(3), 332–346. https://doi.org/10.1007/s10964-010-9534-5

Gray, P., Smithson, H., & Jump, D. (2021). *Serious youth violence and its relationship with adverse childhood experiences* (Academic Insights 2021/13). HM Inspectorate of Probation. https://cdn.websitebuilder.service.justice.gov.uk/uploads/sites/32/2021/11/Academic-Insights-Serious-youth-violence-and-its-relationship-with-adverse-childhood-experiences.pdf

Harding, S. (2014). *The street casino*. Policy Press.

Humphreys, M. L., & Teater, B. (2018). Peer mentoring justice-involved youth: A training model to promote secondary desistance and restorative justice among mentors. *The International Journal of Restorative Justice*, *1*(2), 187–209. https://doi.org/10.5553/IJRJ/258908912018001002002

Hurd, N. M., Zimmerman, M. A., & Reischl, T. M. (2011). Role model behavior and youth violence: A study of positive and negative effects. *The Journal of Early Adolescence*, *31*(2), 323–354. https://doi.org/10.1177/0272431610363160

Irwin-Rogers, K., Densley, J., & Pinkney, C. (2018). Gang violence and social media. In J. L. Ireland, C. A. Ireland, & P. Birch (Eds.), *The Routledge international handbook of human aggression: Current issues and perspectives* (pp. 400–410). Routledge. https://doi.org/10.4324/9781315618777-33

Johns, D. F., Williams, K., & Haines, K. (2017). Ecological youth justice: Understanding the social ecology of young people's prolific offending. *Youth Justice*, *17*(1), 3–21. https://doi.org/10.1177/1473225416665611

Lamphere-Englund, G. (2025). *Protecting children in online gaming: Mitigating risks from organized violence*. UNICEF Innocenti. https://www.unicef.org/innocenti/media/11836/file/UNICEF-Innocenti-Protecting-Children-Online-Gaming-Working-Paper-2025.pdf

Lloyd, J. (2025). The education experiences of young people experiencing child criminal and sexual exploitation. *British Educational Research Journal*, *51*(3), 1201–1221. https://doi.org/10.1002/berj.4116

Longfield, A. (2019). *Keeping kids safe: Improving safeguarding responses to gang violence and criminal exploitation*. Office of the Children's Commissioner for England. https://www.childrenscommissioner.gov.uk/report/keeping-kids-safe

Lopez, V. (2008). Understanding adolescent property crime using a delinquent events perspective. *Deviant Behavior*, *29*(7), 581–610. https://www.tandfonline.com/doi/abs/10.1080/01639620701839401

Maruna, S. (2016). Desistance and restorative justice: It's now or never. *Restorative Justice*, *4*(3), 289–301. https://doi.org/10.1080/20504721.2016.1243853

Maruna, S. (2017). Desistance as a social movement. *Irish Probation Journal*, *14*, 5–20. https://www.probation.ie/EN/PB/0/D0A39BFFC60AB698802581D0003CB6D2/$File/ShaddMaruna_IPJarticle.pdf

McCarthy, B., & Hagan, J. L. (2001). When crime pays: Capital, competence, and criminal success. *Social Forces*, *79*(3), 1035–1059. https://doi.org/10.1353/sof.2001.0027

McGloin, J. M., & Thomas, K. J. (2016). Incentives for collective deviance: Group size and changes in perceived risk, cost, and reward. *Criminology*, *54*(3), 459–486. https://doi.org/10.1111/1745-9125.12111

McGloin, J. M., & Thomas, K. J. (2019). Peer influence and delinquency. *Annual Review of Criminology*, *2*(1), 241–264. https://doi.org/10.1146/annurev-criminol-011518-024551

McGloin, J. M., Thomas, K. J., Rowan, Z. R., & Deitzer, J. R. (2021). Can the group disincentivise offending? Considering opt-out threshold and decision reversals. *Criminology*, *59*(4), 738–765. https://doi.org/10.1111/1745-9125.12289

Moffitt, T. E. (1993). Adolescence-limited and life-course-persistent antisocial behavior: A developmental taxonomy. *Psychological Review*, *100*(4), 674–701. https://doi.org/10.1037/0033-295X.100.4.674i

National Crime Agency. (2017). *County lines violence, exploitation, and drug supply: 2017 national briefing report*. NCA. http://www.nationalcrimeagency.gov.uk/

publications/832-county-lines-violenceexploitation-and-drug-supply-2017/file

Newson, M., Peitz, L., Gitsham, H., Imada, H., & Abrams, D. (2024). "We need community": Bridging the path to desistance from crime with community football. *Journal of Community & Applied Social Psychology*, *34*(1), Article e2757. https://doi.org/10.1002/casp.2757

NSPCC. (2023). *Online risks to children: Evidence review*. https://learning.nspcc.org.uk/research-resources/2023/online-risks-to-children-evidence-review

Piper, E., Ariel, B., Harinam, V., & Bland, M. (2024). The compounding effect: How co-offending exacerbates the harm caused by violent offenders. *American Journal of Criminal Justice*, 1–23. https://doi.org/10.1007/s12103-024-09765-9

Piquero, A. R., Brame, R., Mazerolle, P., & Haapanen, R. (2002). Crime in emerging adulthood. *Criminology*, *40*(1), 137–170. https://doi.org/10.1111/j.1745-9125.2002.tb00952.x

Pyrooz, D. C., & Densley, J. A. (2016). Selection into street gangs: Signaling theory, gang membership, and criminal offending. *Journal of Research in Crime and Delinquency*, *53*(4), 447–481. https://doi.org/10.1177/0022427815619462

Reiss, A. J. (1988). Co-offending and criminal careers. *Crime and Justice*, *10*, 117–170.

Savin-Williams, R. C., & Berndt, T. J. (1990). Friendship and peer relations. In S. Feldman & G. Elliott (Eds.), *At the threshold: The developing adolescent* (pp. 277–307). Harvard University Press.

Smithson, H., Gray, P., & Jones, A. (2021). 'They really should start listening to you': The benefits and challenges of co-producing a participatory framework of youth justice practice. *Youth Justice*, *21*(3), 321–337. https://doi.org/10.1177/1473225420941598

Spencer, C., Griffin, B., & Floyd, M. (2019). *Vulnerable adolescents thematic review*. Croydon Safeguarding Board. https://cbmeforum.org/wp-content/uploads/2023/02/CSCB-Vulnerable-Adolescent-Thematic-Review-PUBLISHED-Feb-2019.pdf

Steinberg, L. (2008). A social neuroscience perspective on adolescent risk-taking. *Developmental Review*, *28*(1), 78–106. https://doi.org/10.1016/j.dr.2007.08.002

Steinberg, L. (2010). A dual-systems model of adolescent risk-taking. *Developmental Psychobiology*, *52*(3), 216–224. https://doi.org/10.1002/dev.20445

Thomas, K. J., & McGloin, J. M. (2013). A dual-systems approach for understanding differential susceptibility to processes of peer influence. *Criminology*, *51*(2), 435–474.

Uhnoo, S. (2016). Starting a fire together: The dynamics of co-offending in juvenile arson. *European Journal of Criminology*, *13*(3), 331–351. https://doi.org/10.1177/1477370815617189

Van Mastrigt, S. B., & Farrington, D. P. (2011). Prevalence and characteristics of co-offending recruiters. *Justice Quarterly*, *28*(2), 325–359. https://doi.org/10.1080/07418825.2010.482535

Vecchio, J. M., & Carson, D. C. (2023). Understanding the role of violence and conflict in the stages of gang membership. *Youth Violence and Juvenile Justice*, *21*(1), 27–43. https://doi.org/10.1177/15412040221116305

Warr, M. (1996). Organization and instigation in delinquent groups. *Criminology*, *34*(1), 11–37. https://doi.org/10.1111/j.1745-9125.1996.tb01193.x

Warr, M. (2002). *Companions in crime: The social aspects of criminal conduct*. Cambridge University Press.

Weerman, F. M. (2003). Co-offending as social exchange: Explaining characteristics of co-offending. *British Journal of Criminology*, *43*(2), 398–416. https://doi.org/10.1093/bjc/43.2.398

Wefers, S., Dieseth, T., George, E., Øverland, I., Jolapara, J., McAree, C., & Findlater, D. (2024). Understanding and deterring online child grooming: A qualitative study. *Sexual Offending: Theory, Research, and Prevention*, *19*, Article e13147. https://doi.org/10.5964/sotrap.13147

Wikström, P.-O. H., Treiber, K., & Roman, G. D. (2024). *Character, circumstances, and criminal careers: Towards a dynamic developmental and life-course criminology*. Oxford University Press. https://doi.org/10.1093/oso/9780198865865.001.0001

Wroe, L. (2019). *Contextual safeguarding and "county lines"*. University of Bedfordshire.

Youth Justice Board. (2022). *Child criminal exploitation: Safe and effective exit—County Lines Pathfinder*. https://yjresourcehub.uk/wp-content/uploads/media/Child_Criminal_Exploitation_Safe_and_Effective_Exit_Briefing_Paper_County_Lines_Pathfinder_2022.pdf

3 Emotions and offending experiences

3.1 Conceptual framework

3.1.1 Emotions as processual and temporally situated mechanisms in child criminal exploitation

This chapter adopts a process-oriented conceptual framework to examine the role of emotions in shaping children's and young people's offending experiences within contexts of CCE.

Emotions are not conceptualised here as isolated causal determinants of offending behaviour but as relational and contextually produced responses emerging within constrained social, structural, and exploitative environments. While criminological research has long acknowledged that emotions influence offending and decision-making for reactive violent crimes, the emotional dimensions of criminal involvement have often been marginalised or treated as secondary outcomes of behaviour rather than as central mechanisms through which exploitation is normalised, sustained, and, in some cases, disrupted (de Gelder, 2017; Loewenstein et al., 2001).

Within the context of CCE, emotional experiences are often shaped by coercion, peer dynamics, fear, belonging, and survival, meaning that emotions such as excitement, emotional detachment, loyalty, and guilt may coexist simultaneously within the same offending event. Existing research has tended to prioritise the role of emotions in shaping future offending decisions—particularly through the anticipation of shame and guilt as deterrent emotions influencing risk assessment (Loewenstein et al., 2001). In contrast, emotions such as fear and anger, which are immediately experienced during criminal events, have received comparatively less analytical attention (de Gelder, 2017).

Crucially, this approach advances psychological and criminological scholarship by foregrounding the importance of examining emotional experiences *during the commission of offences, at the point of arrest, and in the immediate aftermath of crime*, rather than relying solely on retrospective or anticipatory accounts of emotion. Emotional responses are therefore understood as dynamic and temporally situated, shifting across anticipation, participation, escalation, arrest, and retrospective reflection.

DOI: 10.4324/9781003496694-4

Attending to emotions across these distinct temporal phases enables a more nuanced understanding of how CCE is emotionally regulated and normalised in real time, as well as how specific emotional responses, such as fear, emotional numbing, excitement, relief, guilt, or moral conflict, may signal heightened vulnerability, constrained agency, or emerging opportunities for disruption and exit (Leclerc & Lindegaard, 2018; Maxwell, 2024; Nee, 2024). Importantly, emotional experiences within CCE are often internally contradictory, with excitement, fear, belonging, guilt, relief and emotional detachment coexisting within the same offending trajectory or event (Maxwell, 2024; Walsh, 2023). From a preventive perspective, these emotional moments represent critical points at which safeguarding, diversion, and trauma-informed interventions may be most effective, yet they remain underexplored within both psychological and criminological literatures.

Many theories of emotion reference the role of cognition in emotional responses. Appraisal theories define emotional episodes as "processes" whereby factors of appraisal (of a situation), motivation, physiological responses, motor control relating to expressive and instrumental behaviours, and feelings continuously interplay and adapt depending on any of these elements (Moors et al., 2013). Lazarus (1991) theorised that emotions are the result of a two-step cognitive process of (primary and secondary) appraisal and emotional response, including an individual's capacity to cope in the management of negative reactions. Importantly, Lazarus stressed the dynamic nature of such appraisals and emotional responses.

3.1.2 Emotional adaptation, social regulation, and disruption within exploitative offending contexts

Within exploitative and coercive criminal contexts, emotional responses must therefore be understood as adaptive strategies rather than indicators of individual deficit or emotional dysfunction. Emotional suppression, detachment, or neutrality, frequently reported in accounts of offending, can function as learnt forms of self-regulation that enable children to cope with chronic threat, pressure, and uncertainty. Suppressing fear, empathy, or guilt may reduce emotional leakage, enhance task performance, and minimise the perceived risk of punishment or reprisal from exploiters, reflecting processes of moral self-regulation and disengagement (Bandura, 1991, 1999). In this sense, emotional numbing operates as a survival mechanism within exploitative systems, reinforcing compliance and sustaining involvement over time. This interpretation aligns with criminological theories, emphasising the role of coercion and social control in shaping emotional adaptation within chronic offending contexts (Colvin, 2000; Colvin et al., 2002).

Social–psychological perspectives further highlight the relational and group-based nature of emotional experiences during offending. Social learning theory emphasises how emotions are reinforced through peer approval, shared narratives, and collective identity within co-offending networks (Akers, 1998; Akers & Jensen, 2010). Positive emotions such as excitement, pride, confidence, or a sense of belonging may be amplified through group validation, while fear, doubt, or moral discomfort may be actively suppressed to maintain loyalty and status. These emotional dynamics are closely intertwined with processes of training, testing, and normalisation described in the preceding chapter, through which acceptance within criminal groups becomes contingent upon participation in offending.

The criminal narrative experience approach (Canter & Ioannou, 2004; Ioannou et al., 2017) is relevant because it examines the "circumplex" (Canter & Ioannou, 2004) of emotions that an individual experiences while committing a criminal act. A study examining the criminal narratives of children and young people arrested for offences in England and Wales identified three themes (Ioannou et al., 2018): *calm* professional, *elated* hero, and a combination of *distressed* revenger/*depressed* victim. Notably, the study distinguished between *positive* and *negative* emotional states within juvenile narratives. These findings highlight the importance of tailoring interventions according to whether offending is experienced as pleasurable or aversive.

This chapter also draws on forensic and social–psychological research on moral disengagement, which illustrates how cognitive and emotional mechanisms, such as minimising harm, diffusing responsibility, dehumanising victims, or reframing violence as justified, can weaken empathic responses and reduce emotional discomfort associated with harming others (Bandura, 1999). Within CCE contexts, such mechanisms may be actively cultivated through peer influence and adult criminal coercion, enabling children to participate in harmful acts while distancing themselves emotionally from victims. Importantly, empathy is conceptualised here not only as a stable personality trait but also as a contextually contingent process that can be inhibited, distorted, or reactivated depending on situational demands.

Forensic psychological perspectives also inform the consideration of personality traits in relation to emotional processes and offending behaviour. Traits such as impulsivity, sensation-seeking, or difficulties in emotional regulation have been associated with increased risk-taking and reactive offending (de Gelder, 2017). Psychological development can also influence group offending (Gottfredson & Hirschi, 1990). Research has shown that some individuals who are affiliated with gangs or criminal groups share lower levels of impulse control (Alleyne & Wood, 2010; Pyrooz et al., 2013). However, those who possess higher levels of control may require the influence of a delinquent group to offend (Fox et al., 2013).

However, the authors adopt a nondeterministic approach to personality, recognising that such traits do not operate independently of social and structural context. Within coercive and exploitative environments, individual dispositions interact with situational pressures, peer dynamics, and learnt emotional regulation strategies. Emotional responses observed during offending are therefore best understood as products of person–context interaction rather than as expressions of fixed personality characteristics.

Importantly, the authors' approach also attends to emotional experiences that disrupt rather than sustain exploitation. Feelings of fear, confusion, disgust, guilt, or relief, particularly at the point of arrest, during escalation of violence, or through retrospective reflection, may represent fractures within offending trajectories. Such emotions can prompt moral awareness, recognition of harm, or reassessment of identity, even where children remain constrained in their immediate capacity to exit exploitative contexts. Consistent with desistance literature, these emotional responses may function as latent turning points, offering opportunities for intervention if appropriately recognised and supported (Maruna, 2001, 2017).

In this chapter, emotions are conceptualised as fundamentally relational, shaped by group hierarchies, expectations of loyalty, and power relations within co-offending and exploitative networks. By understanding emotions as socially produced, the chapter challenges individualised and judgemental interpretations of offending behaviour and foregrounds the importance of situating emotional experiences within broader social ecologies of exploitation (Bronfenbrenner, 1979).

By integrating appraisal-based theories of emotion with social and forensic psychological perspectives and criminological frameworks on coercion, social learning, and constrained agency, this broader conceptual approach provides a robust lens through which to interpret the empirical findings that follow. It enables a nuanced analysis of emotional experiences during offences, at the point of arrest, and after the crime and how these emotional processes intersect with vulnerability, agency, identity formation, and pathways towards or away from continued exploitation. In doing so, this chapter positions emotions not merely as by-products of offending but also as central to understanding how CCE is lived, experienced, regulated, and potentially disrupted, with important implications for early identification, prevention, and trauma-informed practice (Maxwell, 2024; Nee, 2024).

3.2 Findings

The analysis of the data revealed three key, interconnected dimensions: "Emotions during crimes", "Emotions under arrest", and "Emotions after crime". Each dimension, along with its sub-dimensions, offers valuable insights into the emotions that were experienced during (at the point of arrest) or after committing an offence. These feelings were shaped by a range of influences, including peer dynamics, perceived coercion, fear of retaliation, the outcome of the offence, and the young person's appraisal of risk, reward, and coping capacity.

3.2.1 Emotions during crime

Figure 3.1 highlights the relationship among three categories of emotion during the crime: positive, neutral, and negative. Participants reported *good* emotions as part of feeling *happy* and the crime being *funny*. *Fun* was associated with *risk-taking* and *adrenaline*, which could also be associated with *feeling scared.* These sensations could also be associated with negative feelings of *confusion* and *worry*. Furthermore, one participant described the crime as *horrible*, which stands in direct contrast to the positive emotions expressed. Others reported feeling *alone*, *guilty*, *angry*, and *not wanting to be involved. Self-regulation* was a part of feeling *relaxed*, which for some turned into *boredom*. These findings accord with the range of emotions identified in the criminal narratives approach (Ioannou et al., 2017; Ioannou et al., 2018).

Participants' emotional responses were often shaped by the broader context in which the offence occurred and by an appraisal process (Moors et al., 2013). The same incident could provoke very different emotions depending on the outcome, such as whether the participant was apprehended, whether co-offenders were harmed or arrested, or whether violence was involved. This highlights the relational and situational nature of emotional experiences during offending (Lazarus, 1991). The process of obtaining a financial reward from the offending was associated with positive emotions (Table 3.1, quotes 3.1 and 3.2). Both adult and youth participants (A23 and Y6) referenced thrill-seeking behaviours as part of a range of criminal activities (quotes 3.3–3.5). These positive feelings appear to act as reinforcement, sustaining involvement in criminal activity, especially where such activity is associated with autonomy, excitement, or peer bonding. Participants who described offending as "fun" or "exciting" often did so within group contexts, reflecting the principles of SLT (Akers, 1998; Akers & Jennings, 2019). The reinforcement of criminal behaviour through peer validation underscores the importance of addressing social environments as well as individual motivations (Weerman, 2003). However, one participant reported not fully understanding the consequences of having set fire to a vacant house (quote 3.6), changing a positive emotion to concern.

As noted in Figure 3.1 and Table 3.1, several participants (quotes 3.7–3.12) experienced neutral emotions (relaxed, bored, disinterested, resigned, and self-regulating). Sometimes, this was because the activity had become normalised. For example, participant A28 (quote 3.8) referenced younger people having no fear when stealing cars and selling them on to make money, indicating a process of emotional detachment and normalisation that reduces the perceived seriousness of the offence. Group pressure was also referenced (Y6 quote 3.9) by a participant who did not want to get involved in a fight. The normalisation of offending and emotional neutrality observed in several participants may reflect what Maruna (2001) refers to as "condemnation scripts", whereby individuals justify or downplay their actions. This could be linked to emotional numbing, a response common in youth exposed to chronic stress or trauma. Recognising such numbing as a learnt, protective response rather than emotional apathy is critical for designing trauma-informed interventions that avoid pathologising the young person. Some narratives also indicated that the participant was relaxing at home when a crime opportunity arose, illustrating the power of social media and digital communication (Irwin-Rogers et al., 2018). Two participants (Y19 and Y11) reflected feeling no emotions when

Table 3.1 Emotions during crime in Figure 3.1

Quote #	*Participant A (Adult) Y(Young)*	*Theme(s)*	*Emotion*	*Quotation*
3.1	Y1	Good emotions	Positive	Good in a sense, but kind of, you know
3.2	Y9	Happy	Positive	We were just happy, as we knew we were definitely getting it when we went and met him, because I knew it was a definite then.
3.3	A23	Fun	Positive	Yeah, it was fun. Just joyriding, smashing them up.
3.4	Y6	It was fun adrenaline	Positive	Looking back at people staring at you, like, people who are, like shopping or getting food—"What little bastards they are" and you was like "Oh". You never realise it till you're older but honestly, it was fun back in the day cause you were, like running and you was having a buzz with your mates, but yeah you was acting like a little prick and looking back on it, yeah.
3.5	Y6	Adrenaline	Positive	[I] spotted one of them and my mate slid down it, and I was like, "Okay, there's a quick escape for that". I've jumped on it, slid down it, and it just snapped and went flying off it and landed on my back. I was like "Wow"—I never felt anything like it.
3.6	Y15	Adrenaline Worried	Positive Negative	Buzzing like, just a little kid just having a laugh, innit, thinking "it's a big fire that". Just thinking nowt of it and then when the police come we're all laughing 'cause we got this adrenaline rush, 'cause the police are chasing us and then everyone started getting nicked.
3.7	Y15	Relaxed	Neutral	He weren't a legit guy so we knew he wouldn't grass, innit. So we snuck behind his car and put the thing [firearm] to his head and said, 'Listen mate, take your hands off the wheel, now I jumped in the back and put the knife to his neck and told him to get in the passenger [seat].

(*Continued*)

Table 3.1 (Continued)

Quote #	*Participant A (Adult) Y(Young)*	*Theme(s)*	*Emotion*	*Quotation*
3.8	A28	Relaxed; bored	Neutral	Yeah, it's normally that lot that take 'em. Because like in this day and age, all the younger ones aren't bothered. Do you know what I mean. They've got no fear. So, they just go out . . . do their own money and they turn up with these stolen cars. And it's like "Do you wanna buy this?". And if you say "yeah" then you buy it.
3.9	Y6	Did not want to be involved	Neutral	So I was like, "Well, I'm not getting involved in it". I went, "I'm busy". He was like, "You need to come". I went "Why?" He was like "You need to back your boys", so I was like, "I'll come, but I'm not doing nothing".
3.10	Y19	Resigned	Neutral	Before I was just at mine, like just chilling. Then one of my mate's rung me I was like, "What are you doing?", and that so I told him what I'm doing, and he was like, "Coming out for a bit? We've got a car", so I was like, "Yeah", and we went up to either [Place 2] or [Place 1], we got caught because like unmarked police, so come outside the garage and we got off driving on the wrong side of the road driving as the police, then I lost 'em and the cops was above us, so we had no way of getting out so we tried hiding and they had dogs so it was just like "Fuck it, give up".
3.11	Y1	Self-regulation	Neutral	you don't like, you don't go into your feelings too much, 'cause when you go into your feelings, then that's when you start to fuck up and you'll get arrested or whatever, you know. I don't really know what to say.
3.12	Y11	Self-regulation	Neutral	I had no emotion to be honest with you.

(*Continued*)

Table 3.1 (Continued)

Quote #	*Participant A (Adult) Y(Young)*	*Theme(s)*	*Emotion*	*Quotation*
3.13	Y17	Confused Scared	Negative	A lot goes through your head at the moment, it's just want to get it over and down with cause you get yourself stuck into a situation that you can only get out of, basically, but it's hard to get out of, you've got no one to tell.
3.14	Y17	Scared	Negative	And I was doing that for fear of my own life, it's not something I want to do with my life but I want to do IT and that's what I'm doing at the moment but obviously there's no IT in what I was doing.
3.15	Y6	Scared	Negative	I was like, "It's not a gang fight this, it's a pissing battle, this", it's like armour, and they had knives, stuff like that, and it all—I was like that, looking round me thinking "Is it necessary to have, like, blades, bats and everything, it's not necessary—use your fists if you're having a fight with someone".
3.16	Y17	Alone	Negative	You don't want to tell anyone basically, you can't tell your mum cause what's your mum gonna do, you know she can't come round there just shouting at people, you can't tell the police cause that's not what you're brought up to do, you don't go snitching on your own doorstep basically.
3.17	Y1	Anger	Negative	I don't know, it was a crack-head, they get up to all fucking sorts, they do. But yeah, right, and I've walked up to this car, he's gone "Oh, you're here, your bags are better". I've gone "Oh, right, okay, all right". He went "Go on, give me one of yours". For fuck's sake. My mate's just looked at me. You prick, like that, I've gone 'All right then, I whipped mine out like that and I've passed I, and as I'm passing to him, he's like, "Oh". I was like, "Where's the cash".
3.18	Y6	Anger	Negative	I was just like, I just felt, like, my fuse going off.

(*Continued*)

Table 3.1 (Continued)

Quote #	*Participant A (Adult) Y(Young)*	*Theme(s)*	*Emotion*	*Quotation*
3.19	A21	Worried	Negative	We just sat . . . I remember being all sweaty palmed and thinking like this is such a big thing, yeah. And then there was part of me as well, me childish attitude, actually at the time thinking "Yes! I'm doing it now". And that was the sort of attitude it was. God, you know when you do think back at things, you want to slap yourself now [laughing].
3.20	Y6	Guilty	Negative	Now it started pissing me off a bit, I was like, "Well, he's took the piss here"—see, obviously in three months he would have got a tenner and obviously he was putting . . . got weed and that, I was like "Yeah, there you go mate, you're taking the piss" but my mate was having none of it, he was like "He's took the complete piss" and then obviously, like I said, I felt bad after it, like, its' just one of those things, it's like, you don't—people think if you do stuff like that, you're just, like, a heartless bastard, but you do feel bad, like—I was like, 'Oh I want to apologise to the kid, but what's the point, you're just going to make yourself look an even bigger prick now if you go "Oh, I'm sorry". Anyway, I got involved in that again, but
3.21	Y6	Guilty	Negative	Didn't know I could do that to someone. Cause it was just a clean hit as well, and I didn't expect it, I just wanted to just be like that, he was just stumbling back and—just tell him piss off. It didn't and it just escalated from there and it was—unnecessary is my favourite word today, it was unnecessary, basically. There was no need in doing it, looking back at something like that. Like, I do regret shit, but I do regret a lot of it.

(*Continued*)

Table 3.1 (Continued)

Quote #	*Participant A (Adult) Y(Young)*	*Theme(s)*	*Emotion*	*Quotation*
3.22	Y1	Horrible	Negative	So I went down there and I to G [town], the first place I went to, and basically I got there and I went into the kitchen, and everyone was just bagging up, you know, and the first thing they got me doing was just, like, making it, you know, and I'm in, like, a nitty's yard, and I've gone in, and there's just crackheads everywhere, it's just hanging, yeah, it's just hanging.
3.23	Y6	Horrible	Negative	It was just, it was, like I said, it was horrible.

committing the offence of joyriding with friends (quotes 3.10 and 3.12). For those involved in organised criminal enterprises, suppressing emotions was seen to be an essential part of avoiding arrest (Y1 quote 3.11), but this may also be a coping mechanism (Colvin, 2000; Colvin et al., 2002).

Some of the negative emotions that were experienced during the offence included feeling confused, scared, alone, angry, worried, guilty, and disgusted. There are feelings that are associated with desistance (Maruna, 2001, 2017), illustrating possible turning points or opportunities to intervene (quotes 3.13–3.16 and 3.20–3.21). Only two young people referenced feeling angry. In one instance (Y1 quote 3.17), this related to frustration and blaming a drug buyer, and in the second, the young person referred to his "fuse going off" (Y6 quote 3.18), demonstrating a lack of impulse control (de Gelder, 2017). Two participants referenced the traumas of exposure to drug selling and organised criminal groups (Y1 quotes 3.22 and Y6 quotes 3.23). Self-regulation, as mentioned by Y1 and Y11, was used as a necessary coping strategy within high-risk and high-surveillance environments, reflecting an internalisation of the rules of survival within criminal networks.

Importantly, Figure 3.1 and Table 3.1 indicate a range of emotions during the offence. This is consistent with appraisal theories (Moors et al., 2013), which advocate a dynamic relationship among emotions, responses to events, and motivation. For some participants, emotions were consistently negative. This was the case for Y6, who described several different crime scenarios during his interview. Others (Y1) experienced positive, neutral, and negative emotions when he was describing drug dealing and having been

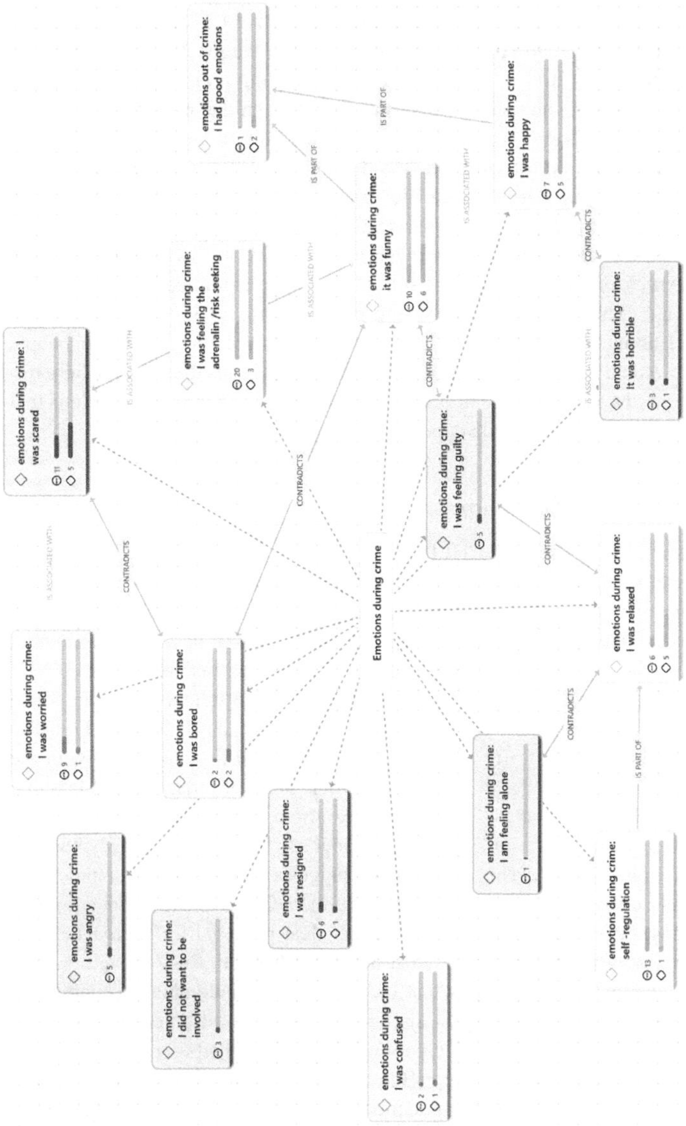

Figure 3.1 Emotions during crime

trafficked. His involvement in crime included being part of an established criminal group over a period of a year, and some feelings were associated with specific interactions, for example, anger at a drug buyer. The focus of Y1's annoyance and disdain appears to be directed less towards those who had exploited him and more towards individuals who were embedded in the wider culture of drug selling, potentially reflecting a displacement of emotion. Although he had left the criminal organisation that exploited him at the time of the interview, he focused much of his frustration on the drug users he supplied. In his narrative, he described them as untrustworthy and "hanging" (Y1, quote 3.22). This finding illustrates the complexity of understanding how people experience the process of offending. It also allows insight into how some of the participants viewed vulnerability and victimisation. While Y1 expressed little empathy for others who were victimised within the system that exploited him, other young people (e.g., Y6 Table 3.1) described regret about their behaviour. Understanding how exploited young people perceive and emotionally respond to their own victimisation, and, where relevant, to the victimisation of others, is critical to designing interventions that are effective, healing, and supportive.

3.2.2 Emotions under arrest

Figure 3.2 (see also Table 3.2 for associated quotations) illustrates the interplay between conflicting emotions at the point of arrest. Feelings of *relief* contradict awareness of *control* and *manipulation* as well as *anger* and perceived *injustice*. Although the point of arrest naturally evoked negative emotions of *anger* (Y17, quote 3.24, and Y1, quote 3.25) and a sense of *injustice* (A32, quote 3.26), one participant shared that he was also relieved that the police had intervened, and he would no longer be trafficked to sell drugs (Y17, quote 3.28). The impact of arrest also dissipated after the first encounter with the police, suggesting that this could be a critical point of reflection and learning (Y2, quote 3.27). Quote 3.28 (Y17), for example, illustrates how arrest can be experienced as a form of liberation, particularly for those previously coerced into criminal activity. This ambivalence suggests the point of arrest may function as a critical moment of potential disruption. Given the nuanced emotional responses described post-offence, there is clear potential for approaches that allow young people to engage in structured reflection. Restorative practices and therapeutic interventions that create space for individuals to name and process their emotions may be particularly powerful. Rather than focusing solely on punitive measures, creating relational contexts for reflection may activate latent moral reasoning (Bandura, 1999) and shift emotional attachments away from the offending identity (including some multi-agency holistic approaches). The finding that arrest was at times experienced as a relief complicates traditional models of punitive justice. It signals that for some exploited children, state intervention represents not discipline but potential

Table 3.2 Emotions under arrest in Figure 3.2

Quote	*Participant A (Adult) Y(Young)*	*Theme(s)*	*Emotion*	*Quotation*
3.24	Y17	Angry	Negative	I've looked, I was annoyed in the heat of the moment, so I was effing and jeffing, [banging] like I said to him.
3.25	Y1	Angry	Negative	Get on the fucking—you know, all that shit—as I've done that, I've turned around and thought, "Fuck". And they got one copper from the other van shouting at my mate, he's just ran off, and then they've just cornered me and I've just there against this car thinking "Shit".
3.26	A32	Injustice	Negative	But [pause] obviously when I've been arrested and I've had my interview and stuff . . . the information's been forwarded . . . they've understood I've not . . . Number one, I haven't got the money to afford the car, although it's not my car. Erm . . . the age I was at as well and maybe [pause] the way I went on. They knew that I didn't
3.27	Y2	Scared	Negative Neutral	The first time I ever got, it was the first time I ever got grabbed and the first time I've ever had a confrontation with the police. So, to be fair, I was scared but after that, it just never ever hit me the same, it never scared me the same.
3.28	Y17	Relieved	Positive	I was lucky, he don't know where I live, I don't know who he is, I didn't breathe a word about anything, obviously my interviews "no comment", nothing like that.

escape (Child Safeguarding Practice Review Panel, 2020). Practitioners must therefore be aware of this paradox and ensure that support mechanisms are embedded at this critical juncture; otherwise, the moment of rupture may pass without long-term change.

3.2.3 Emotions after crime

Figure 3.2 (see Table 3.3 for associated quotations) also illustrates the emotions that were experienced after the offence, including contradictory attitudes of *arrogance* or altruistic behaviour. These were often shaped by a combination of contented emotions, including *confusion,* conflicting *regret* and *regret* opposing *excitement*, which in turn contradicted feeling *calm* and moments that were experienced as *funny*. The range of emotions can be influenced by

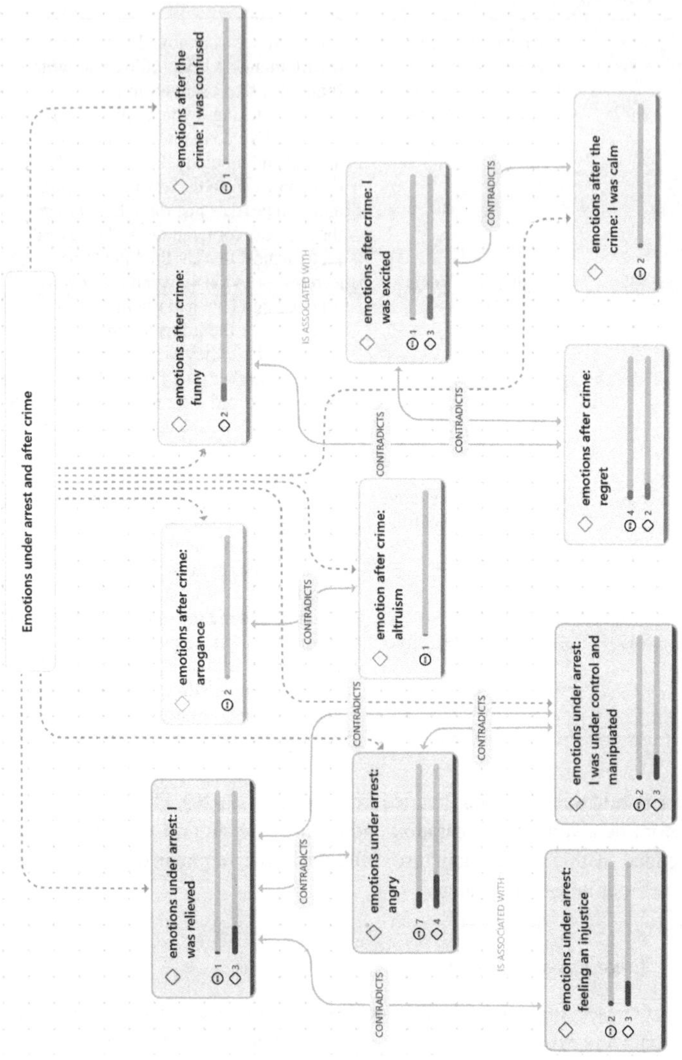

Figure 3.2 Emotions under arrest and after crime

the offending outcome and supporting appraisal theories (Moors et al., 2013). When one participant remained undetected, his post-crime feelings were generally positive (A23, quotes 3.29–3.33). This was an adult who spoke about an incident with ten older friends when he was 13 years old. Walking through a market, the group had noticed that one of the locked stalls would be easy to break into and proceeded to take the window blinds from the shop. He shared a range of emotions, including altruism, which he demonstrated by sharing the blinds they had stolen with people in their community (A23, quote 3.29). Overall, the participant felt that the incident was funny and laughed several times as he recounted the events in detail (A23, quote 3.31). Emotions moved from excitement when hiding from the police (A23, quote 3.30) to calm, as demonstrated by going to find food after evading the police search (A23, quote 3.32). Walking past the police and their co-offenders reveals a degree of arrogance and perhaps further thrill-seeking (A23, quote 3.33). These sentiments were echoed by a young person who escaped from the scene of an arson attack on an abandoned house (Y15, quote 3.34). He recounted that many of his co-offenders were arrested at the site and that his knowledge of the area and quick thinking enabled him to get home undetected.

An adult participant (A21, quote 3.35) and one of the young people (Y6, quote 3.36) who took part in the study shared a sense of regret, but for different reasons. Although regret is typically conceptualised as a negative or moral emotion, in these accounts, it was coded as neutral because it was expressed retrospectively and in a relatively controlled or emotionally detached manner, rather than as immediate distress. Furthermore, regret was associated with the desistance process and the reframing of past behaviours and attitudes. This participant recognised that he was at risk of being caught because of his risk-taking behaviours, and the young person felt that his co-offender's violence and robbery were excessive. They (A21 and Y6) also described moments of reflection that revealed latent moral awareness in the form of regret (quotes 3.35 and 3.36), which were neutral in the sense that they were reflections on a former life. These contemplations highlight the possibility of critical moral development over time.

Three key themes emerge from the data. *Theme 1* highlights that positive emotions associated with offending were typically linked to perceived gains (e.g., enjoyment or income) but could shift depending on the outcome of the offence (Lazarus, 1991). For some, arrest became part of the excitement; for others, being caught transformed an otherwise enjoyable activity into a negative experience. *Theme 2* captures the neutralisation of offending, arrest, and the management of consequences. These neutral emotional responses appear to stem from two often interconnected sources: first, social learning (Akers, 1998) through family involvement in crime, which normalised offending and included an acceptance of arrest as a potential outcome. The second was a flattened or neutral stance (Colvin, 2000) associated with ongoing trauma linked to familial

Table 3.3 Emotions after crime in Figure 3.2

Quote #	*Participant A (Adult) Y(Young)*	*Theme(s)*	*Emotion*	*Quotation*
3.29	A23	Altruism	Positive	The whole community had blinds. It was bad for the shop, but they get a pay out anyway . . . but the whole estate . . . everyone who couldn't afford blinds had blinds.
3.30	A23	Excited	Positive	They sent the canines past us . . . they pushed past us outside and the canines just literally walked right past us. Like sniffed and walked right past. And whilst I'm lying there a big rat went over me, so I had to keep shush. Erm, it's gone . . . the police dog's gone.
3.31	A23	Funny	Positive	[laughing] It's like flat packed as I got on the top of it. That flat packed . . . so crushed down on the floor, got back up, we ran round.
3.32	A23	Calm	Positive	Like his house was just literally like on, after the main road . . . after the street, main road. So, got in his, got changed and went to the takeaway, got some chips
3.33	A23	Arrogance	Neutral	Looking out we see CID unit . . . two lads that we've just been with. Erm, so we're walking past with the chips and I heard them say "If we find anything . . . any fingerprints or footprints in there, you's are going down for a long time". We're just walking past . . . they don't know . . . they can't get . . . we're just walking past with chips and I'm a bystander.
3.34	Y15	Arrogance	Neutral	I thought "Fuck that" and ran home and ran up the field and got through the subways and went home, straight to [home].
3.35	A21	Regret	Neutral	God, you know when you do think back at things . . . you want to slap yourself now [laughing].
3.36	Y6	Regret	Neutral	That was a bit unnecessary, that, taking his phone.

and/or criminal exploitation. At the point of an intervention or among young people without experiences of criminal exploitation within the family, this often gave rise to *Theme 3:* negative emotions connected to longer-term trauma, exposure to violence, and feeling trapped in a criminal group, which can support young people towards a pathway of desistance (Maruna, 2001, 2017).

3.3 Implications for practice

Risk assessment and intervention in youth justice and safeguarding have traditionally prioritised criminogenic risks, with limited attention to emotional experiences as indicators of vulnerability or protection. The findings of this chapter demonstrate that emotions are central to how CCE is enacted, normalised, and, at times, disrupted. Failure to attend to children's emotional responses risks overlooking both deepening coercion and opportunities for early intervention (Firmin, 2020; Youth Justice Board, 2022). CCE introduces an additional dimension to the emotional experiences of offending. Emotional responses to exploitation are frequently complex, ambivalent, and internally contradictory, which can increase a child's vulnerability when they appear reluctant to accept help from authorities.

Emotional states such as detachment, resignation, or emotional suppression should not be interpreted as resilience or indifference. A trauma-informed approach (Darby et al., 2026) is therefore essential because it enables practitioners to interpret emotional numbing, detachment, avoidance, and reluctance to disclose as possible survival responses to coercion, fear, and chronic threat, rather than as evidence of resistance, indifference, or lack of remorse (Home Office, 2023; Maxwell, 2024; Youth Justice Board, 2022). Instead, they often reflect adaptive responses to coercion, threat, and chronic surveillance, consistent with established trauma literature, which conceptualises emotional numbing and dissociation as survival-oriented strategies rather than indicators of coping or strength (Herman, 1992; van der Kolk, 2014). Within contexts of exploitation, such responses may signal increasing dependency and constrained agency, warranting careful safeguarding assessment and trauma-informed support (Branson et al., 2017; Cook et al., 2005).

Conversely, the presence of guilt, empathy, or moral conflict may serve as protective functions, particularly when expressed during or after offending or at the point of arrest. Research on desistance highlights how moral emotions can generate moments of dissonance that disrupt offending identities and open pathways for change, especially when supported through relational and supportive interventions (Maruna, 2001; Healy, 2014; Wikström et al., 2012). These emotional responses should therefore be recognised as opportunities for engagement, diversion, and reflective practice rather than solely as targets for deterrence.

The point of arrest emerged as a critical emotional juncture. For some children, arrest was experienced as relief or emotional indifference, underscoring its potential to function as a moment of rupture rather than a reinforcement of criminal identity. This aligns with trauma-informed youth justice research, suggesting that moments of system contact can either exacerbate harm or interrupt exploitation trajectories, depending on the nature of the response (Branson et al., 2017; Youth Justice Board, 2022). Embedding child-centred, trauma-informed responses at this stage, through multi-agency safeguarding, diversionary pathways, and specialist support, is therefore essential to prevent further entrenchment (Jay et al., 2024). In several accounts, young people indicated that the organised criminal group viewed them as a liability following their arrest, which may function as a protective factor for desistance. However, three young people also reported that, after their arrest, adult criminals threatened their families should they disclose any intelligence or information about the group. Supporting survivors of CCE must include safeguarding them and their families (Hunter et al., 2019). In most cases in the present study, members of the organised criminal group lived locally to the young people, meaning they could access them after arrest.

From a preventive perspective, integrating emotional literacy and emotional regulation into early intervention programmes is crucial. Supporting children to recognise, articulate, and make sense of their emotional responses can strengthen agency, reduce shame, and promote help-seeking behaviours, particularly in contexts where emotional suppression, loyalty, and fear are normalised within exploitative networks (Herman, 1992; van der Kolk, 2014). Programmes that are responsive to emotions such as regret, fear, or perceived injustice may be more effective than deterrence-based approaches alone, enabling interventions to align more closely with the psychological realities of exploited young people (Healy, 2014; Maruna, 2001).

References

Akers, R. L. (1998). *Social learning and social structure: A general theory of crime and deviance*. Northeastern University Press.

Akers, R. L., & Jennings, W. G. (2019). The social learning theory of crime and deviance. In M. D. Krohn, N. Hendrix, G. Penly Hall, & A. Lizotte (Eds.), *Handbook on crime and deviance* (pp. 113–129). Springer.

Akers, R. L., & Jensen, G. F. (2010). Social learning theory: Process and structure in criminal and deviant behavior. In F. T. Cullen & P. Wilcox (Eds.), *The SAGE Handbook of criminological theory* (pp. 56–72). SAGE Publications.

Alleyne, E., & Wood, J. L. (2010). Gang involvement: Psychological and behavioral characteristics of gang members, peripheral youth, and nongang youth. *Aggressive Behavior*, *36*(6), 423–436. https://doi.org/10.1002/ab.20360

Bandura, A (1991). Social cognitive theory of moral thought and action. In W. M. Kurtines & J. L. Gewirtz (Eds.), *Handbook of moral behavior and development, Vol. 1. Theory; Vol. 2. Research; Vol. 3. Application* (pp. 45–103). Lawrence Erlbaum Associates, Inc.

Bandura, A. (1999). Moral disengagement in the perpetration of inhumanities. *Personality and Social Psychology Review*, *3*(3), 193–209. https://doi.org/10.1207/s15327957pspr0303_3

Branson, C. E., Baetz, C. L., Horwitz, S. M., & Hoagwood, K. E. (2017). Trauma-informed juvenile justice systems: A systematic review of definitions and core components. *Psychological Trauma: Theory, Research, Practice, and Policy*, *9*(6), 635–646. https://doi.org/10.1037/tra0000255

Bronfenbrenner, U. (1979). *The ecology of human development: Experiments by nature and design*. Harvard University Press.

Canter, D. V., & Ioannou, M. (2004). Criminals' emotional experiences during crimes. *International Journal of Forensic Psychology*, *1*(2), 71–81. https://eprints.hud.ac.uk/id/eprint/8199/1/Criminal_Emotions.pdf

Child Safeguarding Practice Review Panel. (2020). *It was hard to escape: Safeguarding children at risk from criminal exploitation.* Department for Education. https://assets.publishing.service.gov.uk/government/uploads/system/uploads/attachment_data/file/870035/Safeguarding_children_at_risk_from_criminal_exploitation_review.pdf

Colvin, M. (2000). *Crime and coercion: An integrated theory of chronic criminality*. St. Martin's Press.

Colvin, M., Cullen, F. T., & Vander Ven, T. (2002). Coercion, social support, and crime: An emerging theoretical consensus. *Criminology*, *40*(1), 19–42. https://doi.org/10.1111/j.1745-9125.2002.tb00948.x

Cook, A., Spinazzola, J., Ford, J., Lanktree, C., Blaustein, M., Cloitre, M., DeRosa, R., Hubbard, R., Kagan, R., Liautaud, J., Mallah, K., Olafson, E., & van der Kolk, B. (2005). Complex trauma in children and adolescents. *Psychiatric Annals*, *35*(5), 390–398. https://doi.org/10.3928/00485713-20050501-05

Darby, B., Barlow, C., Heys, A., & Green, S. (2026). Child criminal exploitation and the victim–offender overlap: A trauma-informed reconceptualisation. *Criminology & Criminal Justice*. Advance online publication. https://doi.org/10.1177/17488958261436596

de Gelder, B. (2017). Going native: Emotion science in the twenty-first century. *Frontiers in Psychology*, *8*, 1212. https://doi.org/10.3389/fpsyg.2017.01212

Firmin, C. (2020). *Contextual safeguarding and child protection: Rewriting the rules*. Routledge.

Fox, K. A., Lane, J., & Akers, R. L. (2013). Understanding gang membership and crime victimization among jail inmates: Testing the effects of self-control. *Crime & Delinquency*, *59*(5), 764–787. https://doi.org/10.1177/0011128710392003

Gottfredson, M. R., & Hirschi, T. (1990). *A general theory of crime*. Stanford University Press.

Healy, D. (2014). Becoming a desister: Exploring the role of agency, coping and imagination in the construction of a new self. *British Journal of Criminology*, *54*(5), 873–891. https://doi.org/10.1093/bjc/azu048

Herman, J. L. (1992). *Trauma and recovery: The aftermath of violence—from domestic abuse to political terror*. Basic Books.

Home Office. (2023). *Criminal exploitation of children, young people and vulnerable adults: County lines*. UK Government. https://www.gov.uk/government/publications/criminal-exploitation-of-children-and-vulnerable-adults-county-lines

Hunter, J., Dickson, J., & Allan, J. (2019). *"All of us were broken": An exploratory study into family experiences of child criminal exploitation.* Missing People. https://neurotribe.uk/wp-content/uploads/2022/01/All-of-Us-Were-Broken-Missing-Children-Report_compressed.pdf

Ioannou, M., Canter, D., & Youngs, D. (2017). Criminal narrative experience: Relating emotions to offence narrative roles during crime commission. *International Journal of Offender Therapy and Comparative Criminology*, *61*(14), 1531–1553. https://doi.org/10.1177/0306624X15625991

Ioannou, M., Synnott, J., Lowe, E., & Tzani-Pepelasi, C. (2018). Applying the criminal narrative experience framework to young offenders. *International Journal of Offender Therapy and Comparative Criminology*, *62*(13), 4091–4107. https://doi.org/10.1177/0306624X18774312

Irwin-Rogers, K., Densley, J., & Pinkney, C. (2018). Gang violence and social media. In J. L. Ireland, P. Birch, & C. A. Ireland (Eds.), *The Routledge international handbook of human aggression* (pp. 400–410). Routledge.

Jay, A., Bailey, S., & Geekie, C. (2024). *Shattered lives, stolen futures: The Jay review of criminally exploited children*. Action for Children. https://www.actionforchildren.org.uk/our-work-and-impact/policy-work-campaigns-and-research/policy-reports/the-jay-review-of-criminally-exploited-children/

Lazarus, R. S. (1991). *Emotion and adaptation*. Oxford University Press.

Leclerc, B., & Lindegaard, M. R. (2018). The emotional experience behind sexually offending in context: Affective states before, during, and after crime events. *Journal of Research in Crime and Delinquency*, *55*(2), 242–277. https://doi.org/10.1177/0022427817743780

Loewenstein, G. F., Weber, E. U., Hsee, C. K., & Welch, N. (2001). Risk as feelings. *Psychological Bulletin*, *127*(2), 267–286. https://doi.org/10.1037/0033-2909.127.2.267

Maruna, S. (2001). Making good: How ex-convicts reform and rebuild their lives. *American Psychological Association*. https://doi.org/10.1037/10430-000

Maruna, S. (2017). Desistance as a social movement. *Irish Probation Journal*, *14*, 5–20. https://www.probation.ie/EN/PB/0/D0A39BFFC60AB69880258 1D0003CB6D2/$File/ShaddMaruna_IPJarticle.pdf

Maxwell, N. (2024). 'Shove that. There's always hope': Young people's lived experience of child criminal exploitation. *Journal of Youth Studies*. Advance online publication. https://doi.org/10.1080/13676261.2024.2397025

Moors, A., Ellsworth, P. C., Scherer, K. R., & Frijda, N. H. (2013). Appraisal theories of emotion: State of the art and future development. *Emotion Review*, *5*(2), 119–124. https://doi.org/10.1177/1754073912468165

Nee, C. (2024). The impact of emotion on offender decision-making: Advancing our understanding through virtual re-enactment. *Psychology, Crime & Law*, *31*(5), 574–593. https://doi.org/10.1080/1068316X.2024.2305205

Pyrooz, D. C., Sweeten, G., & Piquero, A. R. (2013). Continuity and change in gang membership and gang embeddedness. *Journal of Research in Crime and Delinquency*, *50*(2), 239–271. https://doi.org/10.1177/0022427811434830

van der Kolk, B. (2014). *The body keeps the score: Brain, mind, and body in the healing of trauma*. Viking.

Walsh, C. (2023). From contextual to criminal harms: Young people's understanding and experiences of the violence of criminal exploitation. *Crime Prevention and Community Safety*, *25*, 282–304. https://doi.org/10.1057/s41300-023-00181-5

Weerman, F. M. (2003). Co-offending as social exchange: Explaining characteristics of co-offending. *British Journal of Criminology*, *43*(2), 398–416. https://doi.org/10.1093/bjc/43.2.398

Wikström, P.-O. H., Oberwittler, D., Treiber, K., & Hardie, B. (2012). *Breaking rules: The social and situational dynamics of young people's urban crime*. Oxford University Press.

Youth Justice Board. (2022). *Child criminal exploitation: Safe and effective exit: County lines pathfinder programme*. https://yjresourcehub.uk/wp-content/uploads/media/Child_Criminal_Exploitation_Safe_and_Effective_Exit_Briefing_Paper_County_Lines_Pathfinder_2022.pdf

4 Self-perception, self-awareness, and the process of child criminal exploitation

4.1 Conceptual framework

4.1.1 Identity, agency, and child criminal exploitation

This chapter examines how identity and agency are shaped within and beyond experiences of CCE. Building on earlier chapters addressing coercion, constrained choice, and emotional processing, it focuses on how children and young people understand who they are, how they interpret their actions, and how these understandings evolve over time.

Identity formation—whether antisocial or positive—has a strong relationship to youth offending trajectories and the desistance process (Jackson et al., 2023). Identity is conceptualised as relational and dynamic, formed within coercive social environments where agency is constrained but not absent. Criminological research on adult offenders has highlighted that the move from a criminal to a prosocial identity is a critical part of the desistance process (LeBel et al., 2008) and is fundamental to understanding routes into, across, and out of offending (Maruna, 2001; Farrall et al., 2014). However, within CCE, children are often framed either as passive victims or as fully autonomous offenders. This chapter challenges such binaries by situating identity formation within contexts of threat, dependency, and limited alternatives.

Social identity theory (Tajfel & Turner, 1979) is also pertinent to youth identity formation, particularly how criminal groups shape a sense of community and belonging during the process of exploitation (Fox et al., 2024). Group membership can make desistance particularly challenging for young people (Amemiya et al., 2017). For instance, Y6 described being ordered to commit a criminal act as a condition of joining the organisation, effectively imposing an identity defined by violence. This identity was used by the adult group members to condition him and to dissuade him from leaving the group. Similarly, Y15 reported being rewarded with a promotion within the group after a successful carjacking, and the more that Y1 complied with the organised criminal gang who were exploiting him, the more trusted he felt by them.

DOI: 10.4324/9781003496694-5

Differential association theory further helps explain how criminalised identities may be learnt and normalised through interaction with intimate peer and adult networks within exploitative contexts (Sutherland, 1947). This is consistent with the social learning processes discussed in Chapter 2, but here the focus is on how such learning shapes self-perception and identity. In the context of CCE, children may come to understand criminal involvement not simply as offending but as loyalty, belonging, work, protection, or survival. Social learning theory extends this by emphasising reinforcement, modelling, and peer approval in sustaining behaviour (Akers, 1998; Akers & Jensen, 2010). Together, these perspectives help explain how children's self-perceptions may become aligned with the expectations of criminal groups while also recognising that such identities are formed under conditions of coercion and constrained agency. These processes were evident in several participants' accounts. For example, Y17 described learning how to traffic and sell drugs after being persuaded it was a "victimless" way to make money and then following instructions to travel out of the area. His experience was short-lived, and as soon as he could exit the exploitative situation, he desisted. In fact, he reported feeling relieved to have been arrested. In this sense, his identity rapidly shifted back towards that of a prosocial student, and he was able to address the exposure to violence and the associated trauma that he had suffered. For others, such as Y1 and Y6, antisocial norms were already embedded within family and peer groups, making the transition from antisocial to prosocial identity more complex and protracted.

Drawing on theories of bounded agency, children's decisions to comply, remain, or continue offending are understood as adaptive responses to coercion and restricted choice rather than expressions of unconstrained will (Evans, 2007; Hesketh & Robinson, 2019). Within exploitative networks, identity is shaped through processes of training, testing, and role allocation, where belonging, protection, and status are contingent upon participation in criminal activity. These dynamics may generate instrumental or criminalised identities that provide short-term meaning and survival value while simultaneously entrenching exploitation.

4.1.2 Self-perception and self-awareness under conditions of constraint

Central to this approach is the distinction between *self-awareness* and *self-perception. Self-awareness* refers to the capacity to reflect upon one's own thoughts, emotions, behaviours, and social positioning (Duval & Wicklund, 1972; American Psychological Association, 2018a). In this chapter, we use this term in close alignment with the American Psychological Association's (2018b) definition of "self-understanding" as "the attainment of knowledge about and insight into one's characteristics, including attitudes, motives, behavioral tendencies, strengths, and weaknesses" (American Psychological Association, 2018b). Developmental and social psychology further emphasise that self-awareness is an evolving and socially mediated process rather than a stable cognitive capacity (Rochat, 2003). By contrast, *self-perception* refers to "A person's view of their self or of any of the mental or physical attributes that constitute the self. Such a view may involve genuine self-knowledge or varying degrees of distortion" (American Psychological Association, 2026). Each dimension, along with its subdivisions, offers valuable insight into how young people view themselves and how this self-view changes over time on their journey to desistance.

For children involved in CCE, opportunities for reflective self-awareness are often constrained by coercion, surveillance, emotional suppression, and immediate survival demands. As a result, self-reflection may be delayed, fragmented, or actively discouraged during active exploitation. This helps explain why many children report "not thinking about it at the time", with insight into exploitation emerging retrospectively rather than contemporaneously.

Self-perception theory provides a complementary lens for understanding meaning-making (the process of how people make sense of events and relationships in relation to the self) under such conditions. According to Bem (1972), individuals often form attitudes and identities within a particular context by interpreting their own behaviours as if they were an external observer. Applied to CCE, repeated involvement in criminal activity, particularly when reinforced through peer validation, material reward, or perceived necessity, may lead children to infer identities such as being "capable", or "resilient", or "criminal", even where these identities are not internally endorsed. These self-perceptions function as adaptive interpretations of behaviour enacted under constraint rather than as reflections of free choice. Importantly, the findings presented later in this chapter suggest that many participants initially relied on self-perception ("that's just who I was") before later reinterpreting their actions through greater self-awareness of coercion, manipulation, and lack of alternatives.

4.1.3 Emotional rupture, meaning-making, and identity change

Moments of emotional rupture play a critical role in facilitating shifts in self-understanding. As demonstrated in Chapter 3, emotions such as fear, guilt, empathy, or relief, particularly at the point of arrest or separation from exploitative peers, can disrupt habitual patterns of compliance and prompt retrospective reflection. These moments create space for meaning-making, enabling children to reinterpret past behaviour not only as evidence of a fixed identity but also as a response to coercion and constrained choice. Social–psychological research indicates that increased self-awareness may intensify moral emotions, including guilt and empathy, particularly when individuals become conscious of the impact of their actions on others (Tangney et al., 2007). Within CCE contexts, such emotional–cognitive shifts can destabilise previously held self-perceptions and open space for alternative narratives of self.

Desistance theory further highlights the importance of narrative reconstruction and future-oriented identities in supporting long-term change (Giordano et al., 2002; Maruna, 2001). In the context of CCE, however, identity change is often partial, fragile, and non-linear, shaped by ongoing coercion, stigma, and criminalisation (Becker, 1963; McAra & McVie, 2010). Identity reconstruction should therefore be understood as a relational and supported process rather than an individual achievement. Taken together, these frameworks position identity, self-awareness, and meaning-making as central—but fragile—mechanisms in pathways out of CCE. They provide the lens through which the empirical findings that follow are interpreted, highlighting how children move among compliance, ambivalence, reflection, and emerging agency over time.

4.2 Findings

The analysis of the data revealed two key interconnected dimensions: "self-perception" and "self-awareness".

4.2.1 Self-perception

Figure 4.1 (see Tables 4.1, 4.2, and 4.3 for associated quotations) highlights the tension between often contradictory self-perceptions and the process of change, offering a critical insight into how support for criminally exploited youth can be most effectively shaped. Self-perception is closely tied to experiences of *group membership*, *peer notoriety*, *respect*, and *confidence relative to peers*. For some young people, *peer notoriety* and *group involvement* offer a sense of *elevated status*. However, this is positioned in contrast to *perceptions of having no status* and *aspirations towards a prosocial identity*, which is associated with *legitimate employment*. Similarly, identifying as *part of a criminal or delinquent group* can coexist with, and contradict, *negative self-perceptions*, which themselves conflict with attempts to develop a more *positive sense of self*. Feelings of *confidence* were associated with perceptions such as *I am not a bad person*, but this contrasted with vulnerability, naivety (*I felt like a dick-head,* and *I feel stupid*), and a *feeling of stigma*. Finally, some young people described a self-perception characterised as *recklessness*, further illustrating the complexity and instability of identity during periods of change.

When reflecting on their experiences of criminal involvement, many participants cited negative elements. A22 (quote 4.1) referenced external stigmatisation of being placed in a particular class at school, highlighting how labelling can influence and potentially limit a young person's sense of potential and future opportunities by influencing their self-awareness (Duval & Wicklund, 1972). For one young person (Y17, quotes 4.2 and 4.3), exposure to violence and environmental risk resulted in the normalisation of crime.

Table 4.1 Negative identity in Figure 4.1

Quote	*Participant A (Adult) Y(Young)*	*Theme(s)*	*Quotation*
4.1	A22	Stigmatised	Erm. I think somebody listening to me or not putting me in the idiot class. Or if you do put me in the idiot class, do it . . . not so everybody knew you was in the idiot class. They just shoved you in a class and left you.
4.2	Y17	Vulnerable trauma	That's not the right thing to know as a kid basically but there's things that people don't see behind their life that we do see, you know it's not . . . you're raised up in an area where crime is literally every day normal life, you see it, just, it's not bothering you. Like you might see someone get robbed, you might see someone's bike get stole, you just don't say nothing about . . . it's just everyday life.
4.3	Y17	Vulnerable	You've got to do what you do for money, so I was approached, just basically taken on as someone who do like, got told what to do, basically.
4.4	Y8	Felt stupid	Just scared, I felt like a dickhead, shouldn't have even been in there.
4.5	Y9	Felt stupid	Yeah, but it was a bit stupid to fall for it.
4.6	Y6	Not a bad person	To be honest, looking back, I am. I'm not, like, a bad guy, but stuff I've done day on day—yeah, I see why people look at me. Does piss me off 'cause you don't judge a book by its cover. All that stuff is done.
4.7	A21	From negative to positive	And then I did every course . . . I saved the document . . . I got it written . . . "completed every course the prison service has to offer". I did everything, everything. I got a diploma, two degrees, I did distance learning then . . . So, I'm a qualified teacher trainer.

The same young person cited a lack of financial opportunity as a reason for his unwitting involvement with an organised criminal group. When asked if he wanted to make money, he accepted immediately without understanding the nature of what he was becoming involved in. In this instance, trauma and vulnerability influenced his decision-making process alongside exposure to a criminal group member (Sutherland, 1947).

Table 4.2 Positive identity in Figure 4.1

Quote #	*Participant A (Adult) Y(Young)*	*Theme(s)*	*Quotation*
4.8	Y1	Identity	And I got good at it, you know, I got really good at it, like, selling it and that, I got a really banging line going, probably doing about a grand a day, fifteen grand a day, you know, I was just smashing it for a while.
4.9	A21	Identity	Well, the reason why I was in that crowd of individuals was because, you know, it's . . . I wanted to be in that group. I wanted to be . . . they had a good name . . . it was all . . . it was people . . . I won't say looked up to, but they had a rep about themselves.
4.10	A27	Group membership	Er yeah because we used to do everything together, do you see what I mean. We done everything together. We sold drugs together. We smoked together. We went out together. We laugh, we done this, we done that. We made money together. So there is that influence . . . the two of us . . . we're bouncing off one another.
4.11	Y1	Notoriety and respect	And I started off, you know, like, you know, not really in it and that, and then as I kind of worked my way up, you know, I kind of got a bit more respect off people, and . . . you just—it's a hard one.

Table 4.3 Positive confidence in Figure 4.1

Quote #	*Participant A (Adult)*	*Theme(s)*	*Quotation*
4.12	A21	Elevated status	It was like . . . it was . . . more . . . it was like a bit of status more than anything. And because I . . . I'm always knocked about with older people when I was younger.
4.13	A25	Elevated status job	It's very organised. It's very organised. It's just like a job like I said. Keeping it low key at the same time.
4.14	A29	Confident	Because it's [shoplifting] a lot easier. And it's a guaranteed thing for me because I was very good at it.

(*Continued*)

Table 4.1 (Continued)

Quote #	*Participant A (Adult)*	*Theme(s)*	*Quotation*
4.15	A23	Confident	Looking out we see CID unit . . . two lads that we've just been with. Erm, so we're walking past with the chips and I heard them say "if we find anything . . . any fingerprints or footprints in there, you's are going down for a long time". We're just walking past . . . they don't know . . . they can't get . . . we're just walking past with chips and I'm a bystander and these lads have just looked up like that and we just looked and he's going 'er . . . fuckin' hell . . . it was mad.
4.16	A23	Confident compared to peers	One lad just jumped out and started grabbing bags and bags of chicken nuggets . . . "what you fuckin' doing man?" We was here for the cigs and the beer and all that . . . "what you doin'?" . . . Birdseye chicken nuggets when there's alcohol down there and cigarettes . . . probably money as well.
4.17	A25	Confident compared to peers	Like I said we got caught because one of my brothers . . . Literally my brother left muddy footprints going to next door's back garden. 'Cos he climbed through. He jumped over instead of going back through the attic. If that wouldn't have happened we wouldn't have actually got caught.

A process of reflection led two young people to experience feelings of deception (Y8 and Y9 quotes 4.4 and 4.5), suggesting that the efficacy of interventions could be contingent upon the stage of criminal exploitation and the extent to which the young person possesses awareness of their manipulation (Evans, 2007; Hesketh & Robinson, 2019). Y6 (quote 4.6) made a clear distinction between his prior period of criminal involvement and his subsequent desistance, expressing frustration that others failed to recognise the transformation in his behaviour and identity. A21 (quote 4.7) described how he transformed the negative experience of imprisonment into a positive transformation through study, thus illustrating the process of identity transformation and desistance (Maruna, 2001).

Many of the young people perceived their former actions and subsequent identity labelling as vulnerabilities and potential obstacles to change. Therefore, focusing on their ability to reflect and their willingness to change should be a critical part of any intervention programme. This accords with the *pathway to desistance framework* (Maruna, 2017, 2016). In the case of young people, the victim/offender overlap and the transition from offender to survivor should also be recognised as a part of this process (Reid & Sullivan, 2012).

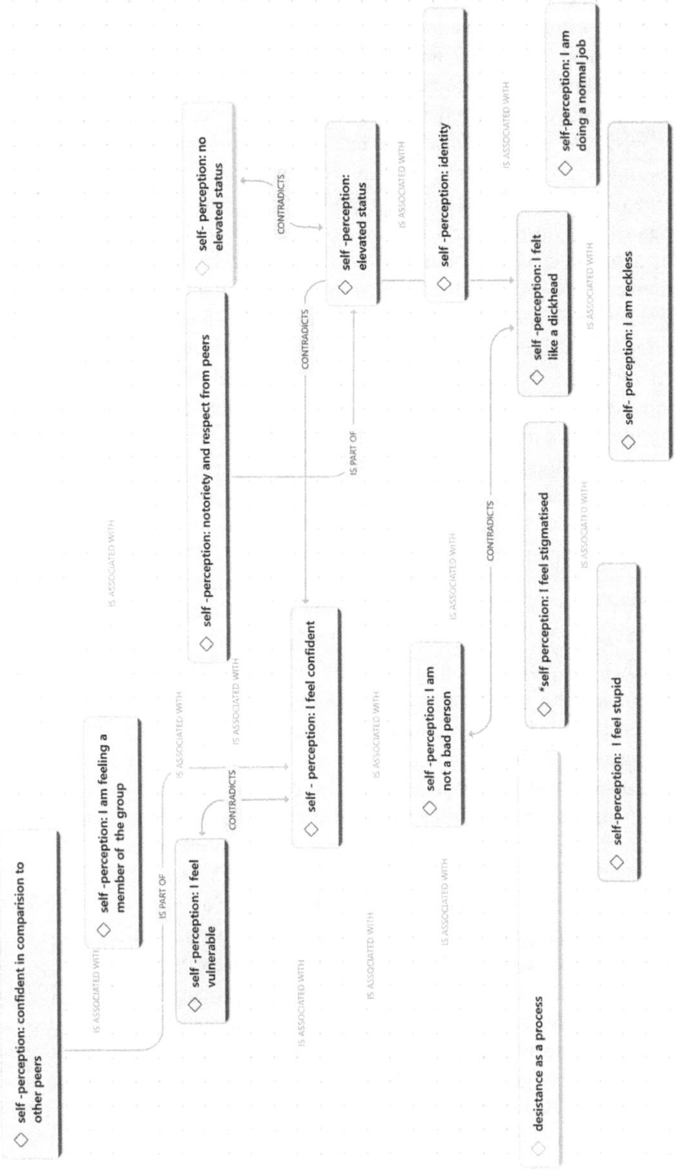

Figure 4.1 Self-perception

4.2.2 Self-awareness

Figure 4.2 (see Tables 4.4 and 4.5 for the associated quotations) maps out a progression in *self-awareness* and was closely related to self-perception (Figure 4.1 and Tables 4.2 and 4.3 for the relationship). Early stages are linked to feelings of abandonment (*no one cares*) and to *family-related* risk factors. This stage also includes confusion about the offence (e.g., *uncertainty about one's role, who initiated the crime, and a sense that the behaviour was out of character*), which aligns with patterns of *deresponsibilisation. Not knowing who instigated the offence* is additionally associated with a growing *awareness that institutions failed to intervene.* In contrast, *responsibilisation* is associated with increased *maturity* and greater insight into the role and impact of *drug use* and *school truancy.* It also involves recognising that the *offence could have had serious consequences*, alongside elements of a *self-fulfilling* "criminal" *narrative.* Although not directly connected within the network, themes such as understanding thrill-seeking (*you want a rush*), recognising involvement with the *wrong peer group, feelings of guilt*, and being *able to talk about experiences of exploitation* also appear to relate to shifts in self-awareness. Finally, minimising the offence, framing it as merely *a mad couple of days*, contradicts *maturity.*

Participants referenced self-awareness through their self-perception as a member of a delinquent or criminal group (Table 4.2). For one young person, drug preparation and sales gave him an enhanced identity and access to money (Y1, quote 4.8). He (Y1, quote 4.11) and two adult participants (A21, quote 4.9, and A27, quote 4.10) shared the importance of the group in terms of their own reputation among their peers through their criminal status. This finding imparts the importance of targeted interventions for young people who have been involved in co-offending pairs/groups in addition to identifiable criminal gangs (Amemiya et al., 2017). Not only is the young person required to change their identity, but desistance also requires a change from group to self-concept. Leaving the group might also be challenging if a young person remains in the same neighbourhood as their former co-offenders.

Two adult participants (Table 4.3, A21, quote 4.12, and A25, quote 4.13) referenced their elevated status through membership of a group with older people. This accelerated transition into adulthood may have lasting effects, as young people navigate the trauma of exposure to violence and the deeply rooted aspects of criminal identity during a pivotal stage of their development (Bem, 1972). For some, success in offending was a source of confidence. When tasked with earning money to pay back a drug debt, A29 (quote 4.14) chose to shoplift because he was "very good at it". A23 (quote 4.15) described how, after stealing blinds from a market stall, he casually walked past the police who were interviewing his accomplices. In reflecting upon a further co-offending incident (A23, quote 4.16), the same participant emphasised his professionalism following a ram raid on a shop. This statement also sheds light on the processes of criminal learning (Tajfel & Turner, 1979). The risk of offending less accomplished participants was highlighted by A25 (quote 4.17), who blamed his younger brother for their subsequent arrest. This quote also reveals a higher level of confidence based on offending experiences.

Reflection prompted a change in self-awareness for both young and adult participants (Table 4.4). Two people described a light bulb moment when

Table 4.4 Self-awareness reflection in Figure 4.2

Quote #	*Participant A (Adult) Y (Young)*	*Theme(s)*	*Quotation*
4.18	A31	Unloved	45 minutes later . . . and me mum said to me like I was something possessed . . . and just walked up the stairs . . . walked into my old room . . . grabbed the bag and when I got to the top of the stairs I said to me step dad . . . I said "what is it that you don't like about me and why don't you love me?"
4.19	Y6	Used by older people	So I was more or less—I was just like, "Wow"—that's actually the most realest thing I've heard ever, 'cause we didn't see it as that—we didn't see it as, like, "Oh, we're kids, so we're being used by the elders to do stuff 'cause no one's going to suspect it". We just thought it was respect. We're part of the family here, aren't we. No, we was basically bait.
4.20	Y10	Used by older people	I didn't, I knew him but I didn't know him at the same time because he used to just, he was from a different area like five minutes away because he was older, he used to come down with all his older mates and just stick it with my group and just chill with us because we were all young, we all had money for drinks and all that so all the olders came to us, just proper using us for our money and think we would do anything for them.
4.21	Y15	Nobody cares	It's just shit, innit. It's just . . . the estate, not just this area, all the estates are fucked in [city] and no one cares about us and that, so that's why we go out doing all the stuff we do.
4.22	Y1	Self-regulation	You don't, like, you don't go into your feelings too much, 'cause when you go into your feelings, then that's when you start to fuck up and you'll get arrested or whatever, you know. I don't really know what to say.
4.23	Y10	Wrong group	I was with the wrong group of mates back then.

Table 4.5 Self-awareness and change in Figure 4.2

Quote #	*Participant Y (Young)*	*Theme(s)*	*Quotation*
4.24	Y17	Elevated status	So, before any of this happened I was in college studying IT, my course was too easy for me so obviously I exceeded higher in the first two weeks of being in college, I done a level one course, went to a level two and I was still ahead of everyone in my class so I was there for like a month, two maybe, and then I dropped out and then I was approached by someone.
4.25	Y17	Maturity	"How old are you?" and I describe myself, I think of myself now as more grown up than I should be than any other 17-year-olds, playing out, going McDonalds, doing what they need to, playing video games. I don't see the point of none of that anymore because I'm more mature, I know I'm more mature than anyone else so . . .
4.26	Y1	Agency	But then I know if I ever went back to that, then I'd end up getting—I'd end up getting caught because of what I've done, and they'd have me on radars and all that—it's just one of them, you just—you've got to kind of make a decision, it's either the money or it's your fucking life, isn't it.
4.27	Y16	Taking responsibility	We will meet or say sorry to each other and that's what we done just said sorry to each other and stay away from each other.

they realised that adults in their lives were abusive (A31, quote 4.18, and Y6, quote 4.19). For some individuals (Y10, quote 4.20), the understanding that adult gang members were exploiting young people developed gradually over time (Duval & Wicklund, 1972). Both sudden moments of insight and more progressive realisation offer opportunities to enhance the effectiveness of interventions and trauma-informed support. Both neighbourhood risk and membership of a delinquent group were cited as risk factors for criminal involvement by young people (Y15, quote 4.21, and Y1, quote 4.22). Intervention strategies should incorporate the provision of practical exit pathways and the development of robust coping mechanisms for young people residing in high-crime neighbourhoods or who are involved with criminal peer groups. Some young people struggle to express their feelings while involved in a

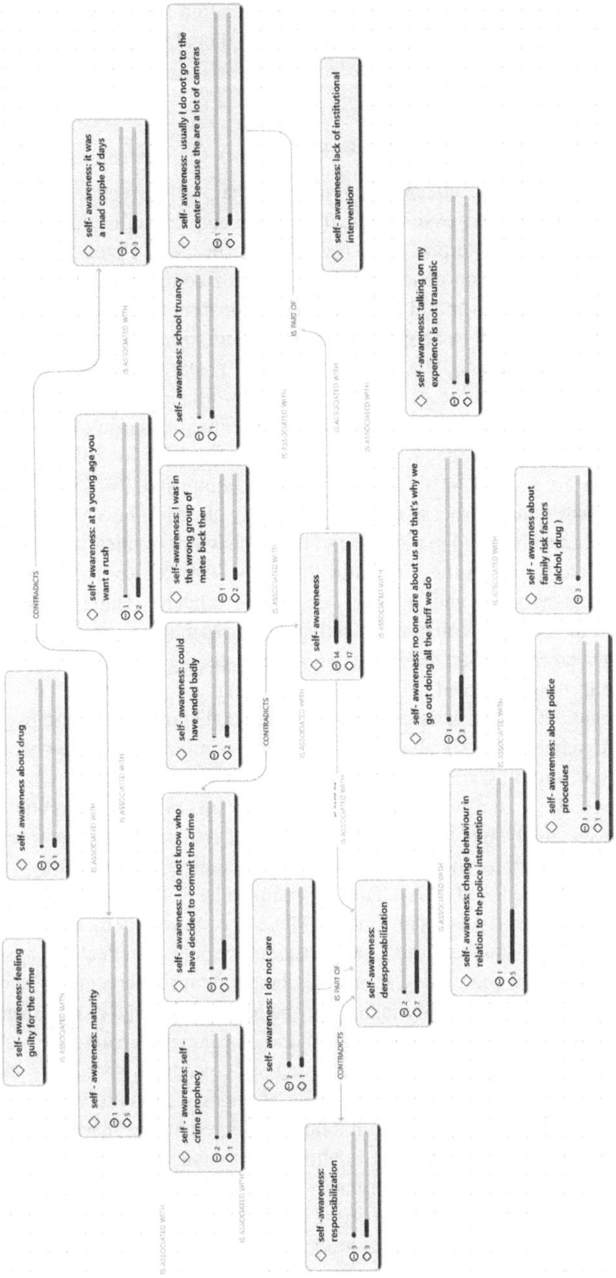

Figure 4.2 Self-awareness

criminal network, as doing so requires them to admit their own vulnerability but may also affect their ability to perform the illegal tasks assigned to them (Y10, quote 4.23).

4.3 Implications for practice

The findings of this chapter demonstrate that self-perception and self-awareness are central psychological mechanisms through which children and young people interpret their involvement in CCE. Practice responses that focus primarily on observable behaviour or compliance risk misinterpreting confidence, criminal competence, or apparent maturity as indicators of agency rather than as adaptive identity constructions shaped by coercion and constrained choice. Recent psychological research highlights that under conditions of chronic stress, threat, and surveillance, individuals tend to rely on more immediate and automatic ways of making sense of themselves and their actions in order to cope, while opportunities for reflective self-awareness are significantly reduced (Vohs & Baumeister, 2016).

First, assessment processes should explicitly attend to how young people describe themselves and make sense of their behaviour. Evidence from social and personality psychology indicates that self-awareness can be understood as a context-sensitive and, at times, depletable capacity (Hafenbrack et al., 2014). In such contexts, meaning-making processes may become increasingly action-driven rather than reflective, with young people making sense of who they are through repeated actions carried out under conditions of constraint (Kross et al., 2014). Risk assessment frameworks that overlook these psychological dynamics may inadvertently reinforce criminalised self-perceptions and obscure ongoing vulnerability.

Second, the findings underline that self-awareness often emerges unevenly and retrospectively, typically following periods of active exploitation. Contemporary developmental and narrative psychology emphasise that identity reflection is socially mediated and frequently prompted by disruption, distance from threat, or changes in relational context (McLean & Syed, 2016). Practitioners should therefore avoid assuming early insight, remorse, or reflective capacity, particularly where coercive relationships remain intact. Interventions that require premature responsibility-taking may be poorly timed and risk reinforcing shame or disengagement instead of facilitating meaningful change.

From a practice perspective, facilitating self-awareness should be understood as a relational and supported process, as opposed to an individual cognitive task. Psychological research on trauma and interpersonal harm highlights the importance of stable, trusting relationships in enabling individuals to reflect on and reinterpret past experiences (Charuvastra & Cloitre, 2008). Consistency of practitioner engagement and emotionally safe spaces are therefore essential for enabling young people to move beyond behaviour-based self-perceptions and towards more integrated self-understanding.

The findings also suggest that early signs of identity destabilisation, such as ambivalence, doubt, frustration with labels, or emerging moral conflict, should be recognised as critical opportunities for engagement. Recent work on moral emotions and self-regulation indicates that guilt and moral dissonance can support adaptive change when accompanied by relational support but may contribute to withdrawal or defensive identity consolidation when met with punitive responses (Tangney et al., 2019). Practice approaches that recognise these moments as psychologically significant can support the development of alternative self-narratives and emerging agency.

Finally, implications extend to institutional and system-level practice. Language, categorisation, and assessment tools play a powerful role in shaping young people's self-perceptions. Psychological evidence on identity development highlights that fixed or stigmatising labels can narrow perceived future selves and undermine motivation for change (McLean & Syed, 2016). In contrast, strengths-based and developmentally informed frameworks that acknowledge constrained agency and evolving self-awareness are better positioned to support adaptive identity reconstruction. Integrating self-perception and self-awareness explicitly into assessment and intervention planning is therefore essential for preventing further entrenchment and for creating the psychological conditions under which longer-term change becomes possible.

References

Akers, R. L. (1998). *Social learning and social structure: A general theory of crime and deviance*. Northeastern University Press.

Akers, R. L., & Jensen, G. F. (Eds.). (2003). *Social learning theory and the explanation of crime: A guide for the new century*. Transaction Publishers.

Amemiya, J., Kieta, J., & Monahan, K. C. (2017). Adolescent offenders' qualitative reflections on desistance from crime. *Journal of Research on Adolescence*, *27*(4), 765–781. https://doi.org/10.1111/jora.12313

American Psychological Association. (2018a). Self-awareness. In *APA dictionary of psychology*. https://dictionary.apa.org/self-awareness

American Psychological Association. (2018b). Self-understanding. In *APA dictionary of psychology*. https://dictionary.apa.org/self-understanding

American Psychological Association. (n.d.). Self-awareness. In *APA dictionary of psychology*. Retrieved August 24, 2026, from https://dictionary.apa.org/self-awareness

Bandura, A. (1999). Moral disengagement in the perpetration of inhumanities. *Personality and Social Psychology Review*, *3*(3), 193–209. https://doi.org/10.1207/s15327957pspr0303_3

Becker, H. S. (1963). *Outsiders: Studies in the sociology of deviance*. Free Press.

Bem, D. J. (1972). Self-perception theory. In L. Berkowitz (Ed.), *Advances in experimental social psychology* (Vol. 6, pp. 1–62). Academic Press. https://doi.org/10.1016/S0065-2601(08)60024-6

Charuvastra, A., & Cloitre, M. (2008). Social bonds and posttraumatic stress disorder. *Annual Review of Psychology*, *59*, 301–328. https://doi.org/10.1146/annurev.psych.58.110405.085650
Duval, S., & Wicklund, R. A. (1972). *A theory of objective self-awareness*. Academic Press.
Evans, K. (2007). Concepts of bounded agency in education, work, and the personal lives of young adults. *International Journal of Psychology*, *42*(2), 85–93. https://doi.org/10.1080/00207590600991237
Farrall, S., Hunter, B., Sharpe, G., & Calverley, A. (2014). *Criminal careers in transition: The social context of desistance from crime*. Oxford University Press.
Fox, A., Fox, R., Linton, C. J., Cruwys, T., Hunter, J. A., Fehoko, E. S., Jones, S., Arahanga-Doyle, H., Winter, T., Treharne, G. J., & Scarf, D. (2024). Social identity mapping with justice-involved young people: Exploring identity pathways to aid the desistance of criminal offending. *Journal of Community & Applied Social Psychology*, *34*(6), e70017. https://doi.org/10.1002/casp.70017
Giordano, P. C., Cernkovich, S. A., & Rudolph, J. L. (2002). Gender, crime, and desistance: Toward a theory of cognitive transformation. *American Journal of Sociology*, *107*(4), 990–1064. https://doi.org/10.1086/343191
Hafenbrack, A. C., Kinias, Z., & Barsade, S. G. (2014). Debiasing the mind through meditation: Mindfulness and the sunk-cost bias. *Psychological Science*, *25*(2), 369–376. https://doi.org/10.1177/0956797613503853
Hesketh, R. F., & Robinson, G. (2019). Grafting: "The boyz" just doing business? Deviant entrepreneurship in street gangs. *Safer Communities*, *18*(2), 54–63. https://doi.org/10.1108/SC-05-2019-0016
Jackson, L. A., Kyriakopoulos, A., & Carthy, N. (2023). Criminal and positive identity development of young male offenders: Pre and post rehabilitation. *Journal of Criminal Psychology*, *13*(3), 173–189. https://doi.org/10.1108/JCP-11-2022-0030
Kross, E., Bruehlman-Senecal, E., Park, J., Burson, A., Dougherty, A., Shablack, H., Ayduk, O., & Moser, J. (2014). Self-talk as a regulatory mechanism: How you do it matters. *Journal of Personality and Social Psychology*, *106*(2), 304–324. https://doi.org/10.1037/a0035173
LeBel, T. P., Burnett, R., Maruna, S., & Bushway, S. (2008). The "chicken and egg" of subjective and social factors in desistance from crime. *European Journal of Criminology*, *5*(2), 131–159. https://doi.org/10.1177/1477370807087640
Maruna, S. (2001). *Making good: How ex-convicts reform and rebuild their lives*. American Psychological Association. https://doi.org/10.1037/10430-000
Maruna, S. (2016). Desistance and restorative justice: It's now or never. *Restorative Justice: An International Journal*, *4*(3), 289–301. https://doi.org/10.1080/20504721.2016.1209253
Maruna, S. (2017). Desistance as a social movement. *Irish Probation Journal*, *14*, 5–20. https://www.probation.ie/EN/PB/0/D0A39BFFC60AB698802581D0003CB6D2/$File/ShaddMaruna_IPJarticle.pdf
McAra, L., & McVie, S. (2010). Youth crime and justice: Key messages from the Edinburgh Study of Youth Transitions and Crime. *Criminology & Criminal Justice*, *10*(2), 179–209. https://doi.org/10.1177/1748895809360971

McLean, K. C., & Syed, M. (Eds.) (2016). *The Oxford handbook of identity development*. Oxford University Press. https://doi.org/10.1093/oxfordhb/9780199936564.001.0001

Reid, J. A., & Sullivan, C. J. (2012). Unraveling victim-offender overlap: Exploring profiles and constellations of risk. *Victims & Offenders*, *7*(3), 327–360. https://doi.org/10.1080/15564886.2012.685216

Rochat, P. (2003). Five levels of self-awareness as they unfold early in life. *Consciousness and Cognition*, *12*(4), 717–731. https://doi.org/10.1016/S1053-8100(03)00081-3

Sutherland, E. H. (1947). *Principles of criminology* (4th ed.). J. B. Lippincott.

Tajfel, H., & Turner, J. C. (1979). An integrative theory of intergroup conflict. In W. G. Austin & S. Worchel (Eds.), *The social psychology of intergroup relations* (pp. 33–47). Brooks/Cole.

Tangney, J. P., Stuewig, J., & Martinez, A. G. (2019). Two faces of shame: Understanding shame and guilt in moral behaviour. *Current Directions in Psychological Science*, *28*(4), 407–413. https://doi.org/10.1177/0956797613508790

Tangney, J. P., Stuewig, J., & Mashek, D. J. (2007). Moral emotions and moral behavior. *Annual Review of Psychology*, *58*, 345–372. https://doi.org/10.1146/annurev.psych.56.091103.070145

Vohs, K. D., & Baumeister, R. F. (Eds.). (2016). *Handbook of self-regulation: Research, theory, and applications* (3rd ed.). Guilford Press.

5 Pathways to desistance

5.1 Conceptual framework

Desistance is understood here not only as a single event or individual decision but also as a gradual, relational, and non-linear process through which children and young people move away from offending, develop prosocial identities, and are supported towards healthy development (Maruna, 2001; Youth Justice Board, 2022a, 2022b; Wigzell et al., 2024; Wigzell & Paterson-Young, 2025). In the context of CCE, this process is complicated by coercion, trauma, stigma, and constrained agency. Disengagement may therefore begin through disruption, arrest, separation from exploitative peers or adults, or moments of emotional rupture. However, sustainable desistance requires recognition, relational support, and credible alternatives to criminal involvement.

In the United Kingdom, CCE is defined by the Home Office as a form of child abuse whereby an individual or group coerces, controls, manipulates, or deceives a child or young person under the age of 18 into criminal activity or involvement (Home Office, 2023). The phenomenon is typically, but not exclusively, associated with modern-day slavery and human trafficking victimisation by organised criminal groups. However, this book considers CCE in its widest sense to include the exploitation of children by family members, often for income-generating offences, which can leave young people vulnerable to further exploitation outside of the home (Ashton, 2023). Even where exploitation involved an organised crime group, this sample was not homogeneous regarding their relationship to offending and so to desistance. Some young people (e.g., Y1 and Y6) were part of an informal delinquent peer group either before or in addition to their involvement with an adult organised crime group (Ashton, 2023; Ashton & Bussu, 2023). Others (e.g., Y17) had no history of offending until they were deceived and then manipulated into trafficking drugs to another city.

Both pathways require the ability to leave the group or control a co-offending relationship. Desistance from criminal behaviours may or may not automatically follow when an individual is able to break away from the group or person who controls and manipulates them. International studies on gang involvement indicate that for some individuals, certain offences increased

DOI: 10.4324/9781003496694-6

after leaving the group, meaning that prior gang-involved young adults presented higher criminogenic risk factors than young people who had committed a felony offence but who had never been group-affiliated (Ashton & Ioannou, 2022; Pyrooz et al., 2010). This was because some young people were offended both as part of the gang and also autonomously. This research also found that juvenile gang involvement was associated with higher levels of exposure to violence and substance use, requiring additional long-term trauma-informed support. In the present context, desistance refers firstly to the ability to leave an abusive criminal relationship and secondly to cessation of offending more holistically.

The gang desistance literature often implies processes of exploitation and control rather than referencing them directly. For example, research has found that the level of embeddedness and/or contact with the group can influence desistance (Pyrooz et al., 2010). Longitudinal studies have indicated that most adolescents are gang involved for one year or less (Esbensen et al., 1993) before selecting to leave. However, one child in our sample (Y17) rarely saw his exploiters because he was contacted by phone with instructions to transport and sell drugs. He reported wanting to evade the group, but he was fearful of retribution and was only able to escape exploitation following his arrest (see Chapter 3). In this case, the young person lacked *agency*, which is seen as an antecedent for change (Barry, 2006). Even where young people believe they chose to be involved with an adult criminal group, their narratives reveal a process of coercion and manipulation. For these participants, desistance involved a "cognitive shift" (Carson & Vecchio, 2015) towards leaving the group. As with the general criminal population desistance research, two processes are identified: a gradual process of disengagement (Pyrooz et al., 2010; Pyrooz & Decker, 2011) and a "knifing off" or sudden cessation of contact (Pyrooz et al., 2010).

5.1.1 Desistance from child criminal exploitation as a conditional process

This chapter conceptualises desistance from CCE not only as an outcome of individual change but also as a *conditional process* shaped by the alignment—or misalignment—of relational, structural, and institutional factors. Building on the analytical foundations established in the preceding chapters, desistance is approached here as a question of *opportunity rather than motivation alone* (Farrall, 2002; McNeill, 2006; Weaver, 2015). Process-oriented desistance scholarship has long emphasised that disengagement from crime is rarely linear and often reversible (Maruna, 2001, 2016, 2017; Farrall et al., 2014; McNeill, 2006). However, these models typically presume a degree of autonomy that is not available to children involved in CCE. In this context, the capacity to desist is constrained not only primarily by attitudes or intentions but also by *continued exposure to coercion, surveillance, and limited alternatives* (Hesketh & Robinson, 2019).

Desistance from criminal activities associated with CCE is therefore conceptualised as situationally enabled. It becomes possible only when changes in relational proximity and institutional response reduce children's exposure to harm and create space for disengagement. From this perspective, desistance can be understood by some as a *conditional exit* rather than a voluntary withdrawal. This interpretation draws on desistance scholarship that highlights different but connected conditions of change. These include the importance of social and structural contexts in shaping desistance (Farrall et al., 2010); the role of social relations in enabling or constraining offending and desistance (Weaver, 2015); the emotional, relational, and identity-related difficulties involved in sustaining desistance (Nugent & Schinkel, 2016); and the need for justice practices to support, recognise, and sustain processes of change (McNeill, 2006, 2016).

Insights from our earlier work on adolescent co-offending suggest that disengagement from crime cannot be understood solely as an individual cognitive shift but must be examined in relation to changing group dynamics and social recognition (Ashton & Bussu, 2023). As young people move away from co-offending networks, desistance often involves the loss of status, protection, and identity previously afforded by group participation, reinforcing the need for relational and supported exit pathways rather than disruption-led approaches.

5.1.2 Disruption, interruption, and the risk of premature closure

Empirically, pathways away from CCE are often initiated through *external disruption,* including arrest, safeguarding intervention, relocation, or enforced separation from exploitative networks. Life-course research recognises that such events may function as turning points by interrupting established routines and relationships (Laub & Sampson, 2003; McNeill, 2006). However, this chapter makes a clear analytical distinction between *disruption* and *desistance.* Disruption constitutes an interruption of exploitation but does not in itself indicate disengagement. Without sustained support, disruption may instead result in displacement or re-entrenchment within alternative exploitative contexts (McAra & McVie, 2010). This distinction is reinforced by Marshall's (2023) empirical study, which demonstrates that responses intended to identify and safeguard victims of CCE may paradoxically deepen children's involvement in the youth justice system. Delays within the National Referral Mechanism and the use of criminalising measures as safeguarding tools can impede diversion and reinforce criminalised identities. External disruption should therefore not be equated with a safe or sustained exit from exploitation. This is especially true of young people who were coerced into offending by a family member, leaving them vulnerable to exploitation by street-level gangs. Such individuals may feel excluded from prosocial networks and friendships and seek out a group that replicates learned family values and attitudes towards offending. A key conceptual risk identified here is that of *premature closure,* whereby institutional systems interpret disruption as evidence of exit and subsequently withdraw protection or support. This is particularly problematic in CCE contexts, where children may remain subject to coercive control, fear of reprisals, or structural precarity long after visible involvement has ceased (County Lines Pathfinder, 2022).

5.1.3 Desistance as relational recognition

Rather than being driven by internal transformation, desistance from CCE is conceptualised here as a process dependent on *relational recognition.* Desistance research highlights the role of social validation in sustaining disengagement, particularly where an individual's past actions have been heavily stigmatised (Maruna, 2001, 2016, 2017; McNeill & Weaver, 2010). In the context of CCE, emerging disengagement, such as distancing from peers or acceptance of support, requires recognition by adults and institutions that do not demand immediate stability, insight, or responsibility. Where responses are punitive or risk-led, these early shifts are likely to be undermined, reinforcing criminalised identities rather than enabling exit (McAra & McVie, 2010). Desistance is therefore not solely the achievement of a new identity but is the *loosening of exploitative attachments*, made possible through sustained relational and institutional support. Recent youth justice scholarship has increasingly highlighted the importance of participation and relational recognition within desistance-oriented practice. Creaney and colleagues argue that involving children meaningfully in decision-making processes can support agency, identity reconstruction, and engagement with support, whereas adult-centric and risk-led interventions may reproduce disempowerment and reinforce reductive victim–offender binaries (Creaney et al., 2024; Creaney & Burns, 2024, 2025). In the context of CCE, this is particularly important, as exploited children may have experienced repeated coercion, silencing, and adult control. Sustainable desistance, therefore, requires not only separation from exploitative networks but also opportunities for children to be heard, recognised, and involved in shaping the support that affects their lives. Restorative and relational approaches can further support this process by creating educational and community spaces in which young people experience recognition, belonging, and participation rather than exclusion or stigmatisation (Veloria et al., 2020).

5.1.4 Supported pathways and institutional responsibility

Finally, the authors challenge individualised models of desistance that locate responsibility for change primarily within the child. In CCE contexts, sustained disengagement is contingent upon access to *material security, relational safety, and credible non-exploitative alternatives.* Where such conditions are absent, expectations of desistance are unrealistic and risk reproducing harm (Hesketh & Robinson, 2019; Nugent & Schinkel, 2016). In this respect, CCE duplicates the trauma of coercive bonding processes that are more commonly recognised in cases of child sexual exploitation and abuse (Reid et al., 2013; Sanchez et al., 2019; Casassa et al., 2022; Reid, 2024). Consistent with Child First principles, effective pathways out of CCE require coordinated, *multi-agency responses* that prioritise protection over compliance and continuity over short-term outcomes (McAra & McVie, 2010; Youth Justice Board, 2022a). Desistance requires a *supported transition*, shaped as much by institutional action as by individual behaviour. Importantly, the psychological harm imposed on children who have been exploited may persist beyond physical separation from exploitative networks and can continue to shape trust, identity, belonging, and future orientation (Moyle, 2019). For this reason, prosocial mentoring-based approaches are particularly relevant because they can provide the relational infrastructure through which desistance becomes possible (Bussu et al., 2024). Rather than functioning simply as individual support, prosocial mentoring can create sustained opportunities for trust, recognition, belonging, and positive identity development, helping young people to imagine and access credible alternatives to exploitative networks (Ashton & Ward, 2022; Bussu et al., 2024; Creaney et al., 2024). For those young people who experience exploitation from within their family, such mentoring relationships can offer the opportunity to view the world from a different prosocial perspective. In the context of CCE, mentoring may therefore operate as a protective relational mechanism, supporting both disengagement from harmful networks and the reconstruction of prosocial future selves (Creaney et al., 2026).

5.2 Findings

The analysis of the data and Figure 5.1 (we have included a selection of quotations from Tables 5.1–5.4 to illustrate the network) revealed five interconnected dimensions that were part of the desistance process: "turning point", "desistance as process", and "the family vs. group", with the latter including the subthemes "emotions after desistance" and "finally leaving the group", which occur as part of the process. These interconnected dimensions are represented graphically in the figure and are further supported by significant quotations discussed across the tables in each section of the findings. Transversally, we also included the dimension of "self-awareness", which is fundamental to the desistance process, particularly in relation to "turning points" (Section 5.2.1). As Figure 5.1 illustrates, *leaving the group*, *desistance as a process*, *family versus group*, *turning point*, and *self-awareness* were all part of *desistance*. *Family versus group* was associated with *self-awareness*, which was also part of the turning point, and *emotions after desistance* were found to be a consequence of the *turning point*. Importantly, in the context of this study, desistance can refer to either *the ability to leave the co-offender(s) or gang* and/or *the cessation of offending or group-related categories of crime*. These two processes are not necessarily concurrent because some co-offenders also commit criminal acts alone as well as part of their group (Ashton, 2023).

5.2.1 Turning point

For those who offend with other people or groups, desistance can refer to leaving the group and/or the cessation of offending. This observation is documented in relation to gang membership, where studies have consistently found that as individuals age, their contact with other group members declines (see, e.g., Bolden, 2012; Carson et al., 2013). It is also the case that gang desistance does not automatically translate to offending cessation, and in fact, some individuals commit more offences after they leave a gang (Ashton et al., 2018). In the present study, which included membership of both formal and informal co-offending groups, group membership and offending were often cited together in reference to desistance. However, it is not possible to desist from something that you have no control over. In the case of young people who are coerced into offending, they firstly need to escape from the exploiter(s) and can then elect to desist from offending behaviours. In this sense, we would not reference survivors of child sexual exploitation "desisting" from this abuse.

Three themes emerged as part of a "turning point": the impact of a traumatic experience as part of the group or offence, a *change in self-awareness,* and new relationships (Carson & Vecchio, 2015). For Y1 (quote 5.1), trauma was cumulative. After being trafficked to a drug house in another city, he continued to work for the organised criminal group who had recruited him, but on reflection of that process, he shared a sense of risk and disgust. Ultimately, he was arrested during a drug deal, and it was this event that enabled him to leave the group and desist from any criminal involvement. As part of that process, he shared a sense of distrust towards his co-offenders and wondered whether the deal had been a "set-up" by one of the group members or the buyer. He had been reported missing by his family, and the point of arrest allowed him the space to consider the impact that his missing status and victimisation had had on his mother (quote 5.14). This case illustrates the profound processes of psychological conditioning and trauma bonding to which young people who are recruited by organised criminal groups are subjected (Reid et al., 2013). For Y1, it was only at the point of his arrest that he developed sufficient psychological distance to reflect and recognise the social consequences of his traumatic experiences on him and his immediate family. This suggests that police contact could represent a critical *turning point* for group desistance (Laub & Sampson, 2003).

The psychological impact of coercive exploitation can be long term. Studies show that individuals are exposed to higher levels of violence after joining a criminal group or gang (Ashton & Ioannou, 2022) and that membership is associated with higher levels of drug use, potentially leading to neurological damage (Ogeil et al., 2019). Participants referenced these phenomena in their narratives. For some young people who had been criminally exploited by gangs (Y17, quote 5.2, and Y2, quote 5.3), experiences of childhood loss and trauma contributed to the development of self-awareness. These individuals described difficulties relating to young people of the same age who had not experienced exploitation (Y17, quote 5.2). Often participants demonstrated a degree of emotional maturity reflected on having "wasted" their lives (Y2, quote 5.3). They also described coping with stress by adopting a clear plan of action to "stay under the radar . . . get to work . . .

Table 5.1 Turning point

Quote #	*Participant A (Adult) Y(Young)*	*Theme(s)*	*Quotation*
5.1	Y1	Turning point Trauma	So, yeah, I was like, Yeah, yeah, sound. He said, You know, you know how to whip good and that, so I was like, Okay, yeah, okay, right, cool. So I went down there and I went to G [town], the first place I went to, and basically I got there and I went into the kitchen, and everyone was just bagging up, you know, and the first thing they got me doing was just, like, making it, you know, and, I'm in, like, a nitty's yard, and I've gone in, and there's just crack-heads everywhere, it's just hanging, yeah, it's just hanging.
5.2	Y17	Turning point Self-aware	It's not nice, you see things you don't wanna see, but just makes you the person who you are, basically, you've just got to get a grip of it, grow up, that's why I'm like when people say to me, "How old are you?" and I describe myself, I think of myself now as more grown up than I should be than any other 17-year-olds, playing out, going McDonalds, doing what they need to, playing video games. I don't see the point of none of that anymore because I'm more mature, I know I'm more mature than anyone else so . . .
5.3	Y2	Turning point Self-aware	And, I didn't want that to happened because I've wasted, not wasted, I've had 15 years of my life and there's no point of putting myself away for it now because that's just ruining it, that is wasting away 15 years of my life if I get put away now, so there is no point in doing it. I might as well try and let myself handle stress of whatever is going and stay under the radar to myself, get work, earn a bit of money.
5.4	Y19	Turning point self-aware	Nowt. I just think it's all stupid now 'cause it's like ages ago but now I've finally started growing up a bit.
5.5	Y19	Turning point Relationship	and I want to stop now because I'm trying to sort me head out for some girl and that. She wants me to sort me head out so.

(*Continued*)

Table 5.1 (Continued)

Quote #	*Participant A (Adult) Y(Young)*	*Theme(s)*	*Quotation*
5.6	A21	Turning point	And it . . . I remember that was a turning point in life.
5.7	Y19	Turning point	Obviously, I had the cornflakes when I woke up and then I went back to sleep. I was waiting for my mum, got interviewed, then went back to the cell for a bit while I was waiting for the others to be interviewed, then went about four o'clock in the morning with one of them and one of me other mates got arrested 'cause he was eighteen
5.8	Y1	Turning point	Not really, no, but, you know, you kind of start seeing people's true colours, you know, say if you've not got money right, you know, they'll go mad and they'll try and, like, slap you or something, and you're like, Oh, you know, and you'll get in a little brawl with them, and then it'll end out that they've worked out something wrong and then it's Oh, sorry brother, you know, all that shit, but it's an odd one. It's all about money, that's all it is, you know, they don't give a shit about you, it's all about money. That's all it is.

earn a bit of money [legitimately]". Others referenced "growing up" (Carson & Vecchio, 2015) and "sorting [their] head out" (Y19, quotes 5.4 and 5.5). In many respects, these young people are articulating what one of the adult participants (A21, quote 5.6) identified as a significant "turning point" in their pathway to desistance. Such statements emphasise the need for longer-term, trauma-informed support for young people who have been criminally exploited. They also highlight the importance of determining an appropriate intensity and type of intervention that aligns with a survivor's specific needs at each stage of their desistance journey. For example, Y19 (quote 5.7) reported feeling calm and relaxed following his arrest (Chapter 3) and questioning at a police station, a response that occurred while he was actively embedded within a criminal network. His turning point emerged later, after he started a new relationship, when his girlfriend signalled the need for him to "sort his head out" (Y19, quote 5.5). Turning points may arise from cumulative experiences, especially when a person recognises that they are being abused (Y1, quote 5.8): "they don't give a shit about you". Y1 (quote 5.8) described an incident during which his exploiter claimed he had not handed over all the drug money; after beating him, the exploiter found the missing amount and apologised. This is an example of trauma bonding whereby criminals intersperse gifts with fear, dependency, and compliance to control a victim of sexual or criminal exploitation (Reid, 2024).

5.2.2 *Desistance as a process*

Consistent with wider desistance scholarship (Farrall et al., 2014; Maruna, 2001, 2016, 2017; McNeill, 2006), Y19 described a gradual withdrawal from co-offending (Q5.9). For this participant, involvement in episodes where friends had stolen a vehicle and his participation in subsequent police chases functioned as a source of excitement, risk-taking, and reinforced his social bonds with his peers. In his narrative, he distinguished between this type of sensory offending and what he considered more serious income-generating behaviours. Although Y7 was clear that isolated police interventions were not part of the desistance process (quote 5.10), being known to the authorities could act as a deterrent to continued involvement with a gang or organised criminal group (Ashton, 2023). An adult participant (A21, quote 5.11) described the process of "ageing out" of both offending and group exploitation, framing this transition as an increased awareness of the personal, social, and emotional losses experienced after arrest and sentencing. Another adult, who had sold drugs within a peer group to fund his own use during

Table 5.2 Process-oriented desistance in Figure 5.1

Quote #	*Participant A (Adult) Y(Young)*	*Theme(s)*	*Quotation*
5.9	Y19	Process	Obviously, I go and get in stolen cars and that and I take a few police chases but not as much as I used to.
5.10	Y7	Process	Not a deterrent in general, just for that place.
5.11	A21	Process	Once you decide the loss . . . and I think it's age as well. I think I must have been a late developer, because it terms of maturity. So, erm.
5.12	A27	Change	You know what, you've just said that. Times have changed. You're talking . . . talking at least . . . say around . . . 10, 15 years. . . . Now, I wouldn't know because I don't do it. I work for a living and that . . . I don't drink . . . I don't smoke . . . so all that is redundant to me. And what I do . . . I still know the processes . . . ounces . . . half ounce . . . quarters . . . eighths . . . I still know that process . . . don't know the prices because from since then, everything changes. I don't even wish to know to tell you the truth.

adolescence, explained that desistance involved a loss of situational knowledge (A27 quote 5.12), specifically, no longer knowing the cost of drugs. This observation demonstrates a loss of group and offending knowledge, especially because the participant differentiates between knowledge of the process (retained) and knowledge of the cost of drugs (lost).

5.2.3 The group versus family

Family can operate as both a risk and a protective factor in the criminal exploitation of a young person (Fox et al., 2024; Maxwell, 2023). Several participants noted that either their own relative or a family relative connected through a peer was responsible for recruiting or coercing them into a criminal group (see Chapter 2). The presence of such an influence may constitute an additional barrier

Table 5.3 The group versus family in Figure 5.1

Quote #	*Participant A (Adult) Y(Young)*	*Theme(s)*	*Quotation*
5.13	A32	Family	Yeah. Yeah, actually I did. Erm [pauses]. I was . . . I was friends with . . . up until a bit after that. But a wrath come between us. And obviously, the [co-offender's] relative . . . I didn't speak to him again. So, erm . . . yeah it just
5.14	Y1	Family	You've got to kind of make a decision, it's either the money or it's your fucking life, isn't it, you know, and my family, like, when I was away, I went missing, you know, and my mam, she, like, she fainted outside the Co-op [shop] and all that, you know, like proper over when I got back, kind of seeing the destruction doing it, kind of makes you feel like you shouldn't.
5.15	Y17	Family	That's because [pause] it's hard to describe, but your mum's your mum at the end of the day, your mum's going to have your back at the end, everything like . . . when I got arrested my mum, any other mum would have turned their back and just dropped, didn't want to know, my mum stuck with me through everything and she helped me not be in jail, not be still in trouble with that person, not being doing anything like that, like yeah . . .
5.16	Y20	Family	Yeah, I had to—I had to do—there's some money missing, and then my dad had to pay them back. I had to—I think there was four hundred pounds missing. I had to do them odd jobs in the house, which was a long time, like a load of washing the cars.

that complicates the process of escaping a criminal group (Ashton, 2023). For A32, he severed ties with the older family member of a peer who had given him a stolen car before he cut ties with his friend (quote 5.13). Importantly, families were cited by several adult and adolescent interviewees as supporting their desistance (quotes 5.13–16). Y1 and Y17 referenced the impact of being trafficked on their mothers and acknowledged the support that they were given following their arrests. In this sense, the family played a critical role in supporting them to break away from the criminal group and in helping them towards a new identity (Fox et al., 2024). For Y20 (quote 5.16), his father not only paid off his debt but also taught him the value of repaying this money through helping with chores. Thus, he actively teaches his son an alternative way to make money by working rather than through theft. Parental support, or lack of, is an important factor for youth desistance from a social and psychological standpoint.

Following his arrest, Y1 (quote 5.14) described how he was released from the drug debt he owed on account of the arrest and how he was effectively dismissed by the group, on condition that he did not disclose any information to the police. He also reported that his former trafficker threatened to shoot him and his mother. This account is important because it demonstrates that leaving a criminal group is possible, particularly in situations such as Y1's, where an individual becomes less valuable to the group once they are known to the police. However, the threats directed towards Y1 and his family are likely to contribute to longer-term anxiety. This is especially relevant given his account of being assaulted by street-level gang members, who justified the violence by claiming that Y1 had pocketed some of the drug money before admitting he had miscounted the notes (Y1 quote 5.8).

Y6 described an alternative group desistance process. He was not trafficked, but he did suffer a cycle of abuse and forced involvement in violence, which was associated with PTSD and severe anxiety (D'Andrea et al., 2012). To avoid the gang members, he claimed that he was ill and stayed at home, and when this worked as a tactic, he told people that he had started a new relationship and did not want to continue to be a part of the group, thus referencing a relationship turning point to leave the group. Like Y1, he was also threatened with violence, but he argued that his own (forced) involvement in crimes meant that reporting the group would only incriminate himself.

For other participants, not knowing any details about those responsible for their trafficking helped with escaping the group (Y17 quote 5.19). Y17 was instructed to travel over 200 miles by train each day to sell drugs. The original recruitment process involved considerable deception, and the young person found himself trapped in a criminal organisation. He was eventually arrested, and this turning point enabled him to break away from the organised criminal group that had recruited him because he had no detailed knowledge of the group or its members. Support following these experiences is critical for young people, as highlighted by Y19 (quote 5.20), who was one of several

Table 5.4 Leaving the group in Figure 5.1

Quote #	*Participant A (Adult) Y(Young)*	*Theme(s)*	*Quotation*
5.17	Y1	Leaving the group	And he just said to me, Don't worry about it, you know, 'cause obviously I got some gear took off me, and he was, you know, Don't worry about it and that. Obviously, he just said "Don't say a name, you know, 'cause—fucking, do you know, I'll come to your house, and I'll shoot your mam, and I'll shoot you, and I'll shoot"—you know, all that shit. It was all like that, literally, it was—literally like that, and I knew it would have happened, you know. It was like, "if you say one name, anyone gets arrested, you know, I'm coming to your house, I know where you live and I'm going to blast your face off, you know, after I've blasted your mum's", you know what I mean.
5.18	Y10	Desistance Leaving the group	It weren't like it was like that. It took me a few weeks of having to actually describe myself, I just had to say I was ill for a bit to stop me from going out but then I thought I weren't even going to lie any more. I just went I've got a bird and I'm changing my priorities and then that started it all like you're a dickhead, we're going to batter you and that.
5.19	Y17	Desistance Leaving the group New life	I openly admit I don't know the guy's name, just know a catch name for him, but that's just, I've just left it as that, I just don't speak about it, just go to work, come back and stuff like that, but there's nothing major about it.
5.20	Y19	Support	Yeah, D's [youth worker] been helping me a lot, he's been talking to me about everything.

young people to reference their youth worker in their narratives. Having access to a safe relationship where young people who have been criminally exploited can be supported emotionally and psychologically by professionals, and where they can explore an alternative identity, is a critical desistance aid.

5.2.4 Case study

A consistent theme to emerge from the adult and youth narratives in this study was a life *turning point*, often occurring due to *external disruption* (Laub & Sampson, 2003), resulting in the participant's release from the control of a group or co-offender. Table 5.5 contains excerpts from a case study of an adult who had joined a criminal group during adolescence (A21) for social status and who became the junior member of an armed robbery group that targeted cash-in-transit companies. This participant overcame a long sentence, incarceration, and the breakdown of a relationship to create a new career pathway and identity (quotes 5.21 and 5.25). Although his initial contact with the organised criminal group had been voluntary, he was instructed and told to take part in violent offending. The main reason for continuing his involvement as an adult was the large amounts of money he earned as part of the group. In this respect, his arrest had not been a positive turning point. Nevertheless, his incarceration allowed him to train for a legitimate career path and desist from the group and offending.

The *exploitation–desistance journey* illustrates the journey through which children may become involved in, conditioned, embedded within, and, in some

Table 5.5 Case study of the desistance process

Quote #	*Participant A (Adult) Y(Young)*	*Theme(s)*	*Quotation*
5.21	A21	Sentencing	Well, I went prison. I spent a total 16 years in prison. Er, I got three eight-year sentences back-to-back for armed robberies.
5.22	A21	Turning point	I was sitting on me bed, me cell bed, er . . . I was on basics, didn't have TV, no electrics. It was just . . . I thought I'm better than this, I'm worth more than this.
5.23	A21	Turning point	Me Missus at the time left me after 13 years, which I didn't blame her.
5.24	A21	Turning point	So I thought "right, what am I going to do" . . . I wanted to get a plan now for when I come home. So when I passed me teachers [exam] . . . I couldn't believe it, I was dead excited.
5.25	A21	New identity	I've been mentoring about eight years now. So around that time I become a mentor. There was an A4 piece of paper up on the wall and I was only on 45p a day . . . wages yeah. It was just an A4 piece of paper, doing a survey to get food . . . mentors wanted twenty pound a week. I'll be honest with you when I saw twenty pound a week, I thought great, I'll go for that. Went for that. Went to the chapel. Sat there with about a dozen lads, going through [it]. We was all laughing, a bit nervous, sceptical and so on. Took to it like a duck to water and, er, ended up facilitating life concessions at eight different prisons every single day. Just got thrown in at the deep end. The feedback off the lads was great. In fact, I never . . . I was pretty good at coming back in a positive way

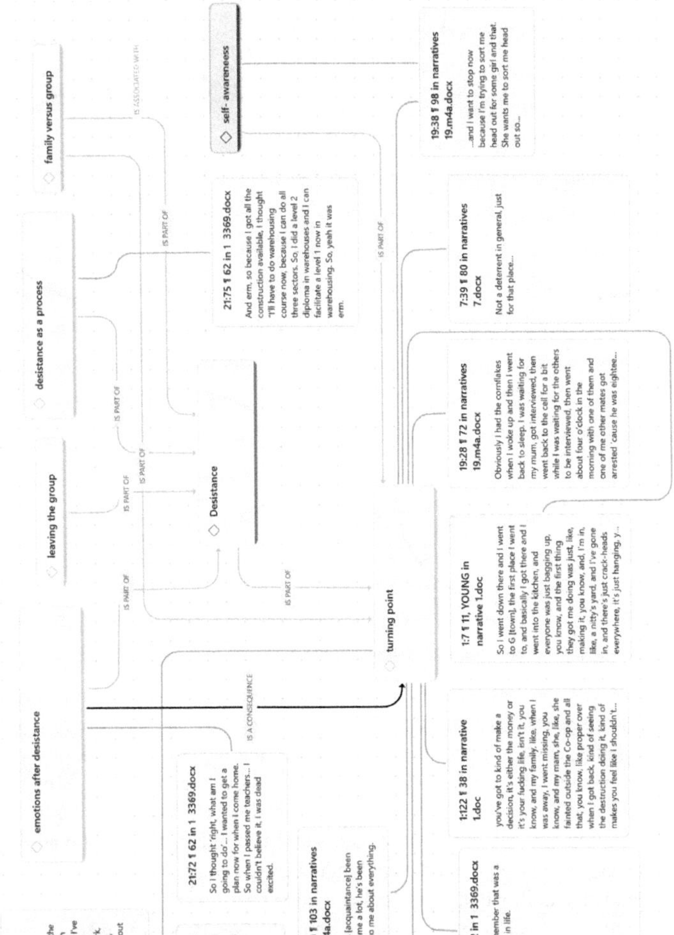

Figure 5.1 Pathways to desistance

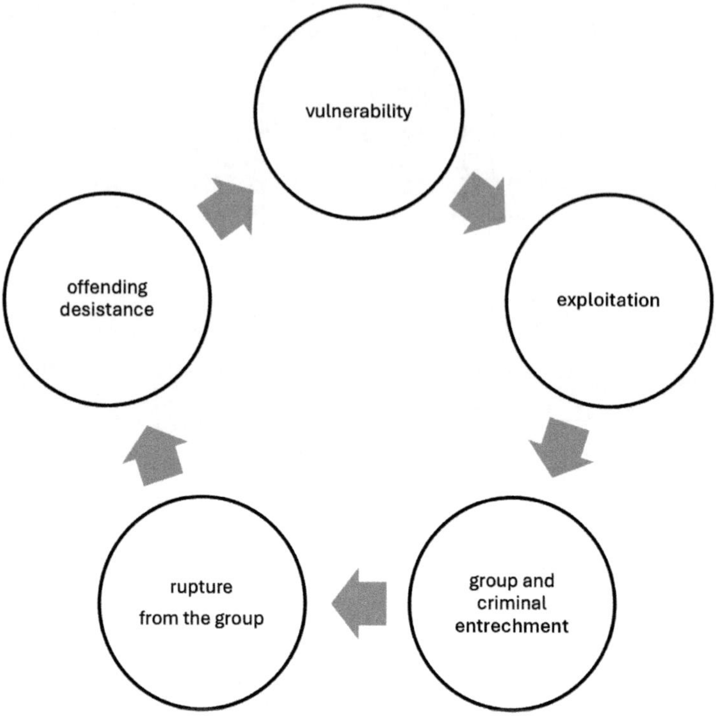

Figure 5.2 Exploitation–Desistance Journey in Child Criminal Exploitation

cases, disengage from criminal exploitation. The *exploitation–desistance journey* is presented as circular rather than linear, reflecting the empirical findings presented throughout this book, which show that children's experiences of exploitation rarely follow a straightforward or irreversible path. Movement between phases is often uneven, interrupted, and shaped by relational, emotional, and structural conditions rather than by individual choice alone. It also highlights the continued vulnerability that persists after a young person has desisted.

The journey typically begins with *vulnerability*, understood as a set of overlapping circumstances that increase exposure to harm. These include structural disadvantage, family and relational adversity, educational exclusion, undiagnosed or untreated cognitive disorders or mental illness, exposure to violence, ACEs, and social marginalisation (Maxwell et al., 2019). For practitioners, this phase highlights the importance of recognising vulnerability as contextual and cumulative, rather than as an individual failing or risk factor in isolation.

Exploitation develops through relational processes that are often gradual and emotionally embedded. Children may initially experience involvement as protective, mutually beneficial, or normalised, particularly where exploitative relationships offer belonging, recognition, or material gain. This psychological conditioning helps explain why children may not disclose harm, may resist professional intervention, or may appear agentic despite being subject to coercive control (Marshall, 2024; Maxwell, 2026). This last point is demonstrated by the case study in Table 5.5, where A21 described his initial attraction to the group and his subsequent involvement in armed robberies as an adolescent.

As involvement deepens, the journey may move into *entrenchment*. At this stage, exploitation is sustained through fear, dependency, emotional suppression, debt, loyalty expectations, and limited perceived alternatives. Crucially, entrenchment is also reinforced through peer training and social learning, whereby children are exposed to the acquisition of criminal skills and the normalisation of antisocial attitudes and are controlled by more experienced peers or older associates within exploitative networks. This process normalises offending behaviour, strengthens group identity, and increases functional dependence on the group, further narrowing perceived routes of exit. Entrenchment does not reflect increased criminal commitment but rather a narrowing of choice within coercive environments. For practitioners, this phase underscores why exit is rarely immediate or self-initiated and why punitive or disruption-focused responses may exacerbate harm.

Rupture refers to moments of disruption within this journey. These may include emotional crises, experiences of betrayal, arrest-related relief, exposure to violence, or enforced separation from exploitative networks. Rupture creates a potential opening for change but remains fragile and unstable. Without appropriate support, children may return to earlier phases of exploitation. This can also refer to leaving the group.

Desistance is therefore conceptualised as a supported, relational, and non-linear process, rather than a final end-point. Movement towards disengagement depends on safety, trust, sustained relational support, and access to meaningful alternatives to criminal involvement. The circular structure of the process recognises that desistance can be partial, temporary, or interrupted, particularly where underlying vulnerabilities and coercive relationships remain unaddressed. Desistance may refer to disengagement from the social group or to the cessation of maladaptive or antisocial behaviours. However, these processes are distinct and do not necessarily coincide, and young people require support on their journey.

Overall, this journey offers a shared framework for academics and practitioners to understand how exploitation unfolds over time, why children may remain involved despite harm, and where intervention is most likely to be effective. By emphasising process, relational dynamics, and constrained agency, the model moves beyond binary distinctions between victimhood and offending and supports child-centred, trauma-informed, and prevention-oriented responses to CCE.

5.3 Implications for practice

Offending and gang desistance literature implies agency and choice, neither of which may be available to young people who have been criminally exploited. The process of CCE shares important similarities with Child Sexual Abuse and Exploitation (CSAE; Reid, 2024), and yet there are considerable differences in the language used to describe the cessation of these two forms of abuse. Young people may not fully comprehend the process of being exploited because of psychological manipulation and entrenchment. They are likely to require considerable psychological support as they begin to recognise their experiences as atypical for their age. Furthermore, professionals need to understand that the young person and their family could be in perceived or real danger from criminal groups. In this respect, the point of arrest can be critical as either a starting point or an opportunity to escape from exploiters and the associated offences (Darby et al., 2026; Jay et al., 2024). Law enforcement can play a critical role, particularly for those who have been exploited within their family from a young age.

Consistent with the theoretical framework developed throughout this chapter, practice responses should recognise that many children involved in CCE occupy a complex position as both individuals involved in harmful or criminalised behaviours and victims of coercion, manipulation, and exploitation (Firmin, 2020; Haines & Case, 2015; Marshall, 2023). Interventions should therefore move beyond narrow offender-focused approaches and instead prioritise safeguarding, trauma-informed support, relational stability, and longer-term social inclusion (McNeill, 2006; Weaver, 2016). This is particularly important given that children's capacity to disengage from exploitation is often shaped not simply by motivation but by the availability of safe relationships, supportive interventions, and realistic opportunities for reintegration and recovery.

The exploitation-to-desistance journey (Figure 5.2) can be a useful guide to identifying appropriate interventions, according to where a young person is in the process. Identifying vulnerabilities both before the exploitation occurs and after desistance from involvement is critical for both prevention and intervention. Supporting adolescents during the entrenchment stage may help disrupt the progression of exploitation and reduce further harm. Although movement from the *entrenchment* stage to *rupture* may create a particularly important opportunity for effective intervention, support should not be delayed until the *rupture* stage. Instead, interventions should be available throughout the process and adapted to the young person's safety, needs, readiness, and level of engagement. Young people who have experienced exploitation remain vulnerable to further coercion and may require additional, long-term support to address trauma and exposure to violence. Interventions should therefore adopt long-term and relational approaches, rather than assuming that disengagement represents a complete or stable exit from exploitation. Nor does cessation of group membership necessarily result in desistance from offending (Ashton et al., 2018).

Restorative approaches are particularly important in school and educational settings, where they can support inclusion, strengthen belonging, reduce exclusionary responses, and create relational spaces that may help prevent children's vulnerability to exploitation (Bussu et al., 2018; Veloria et al., 2020).

Such approaches are particularly relevant within the context of CCE, where school exclusion, social marginalisation, and weakened relational support may increase vulnerability to exploitation and further entrenchment within harmful networks.

This is directly relevant to desistance from CCE, as educational inclusion, positive relationships, and a sense of belonging can provide children with alternative sources of identity, recognition, and support outside exploitative networks. Relational and restorative approaches (Hopkins, 2024) may therefore contribute not only to prevention but also to longer-term disengagement and recovery, by supporting accountability, dialogue, and relational repair, provided that such interventions remain voluntary, carefully risk-assessed, and attentive to victims' needs, safety, and experiences (Bussu & Karp, 2025, 2026a, 2026b). Desistance in the form of escaping a criminal group may not necessarily align with the complete cessation of offending behaviours for some young people. Participants reported continuing offences that were perceived as sensory-seeking or excitement-driven, such as joyriding, even after they had disengaged from the criminal group. This further highlights the complexity and non-linearity of desistance processes within the context of CCE and reinforces the importance of ongoing support, relational stability, and long-term intervention beyond the point of immediate disengagement.

References

Ashton, S. A. (2023). *Pathways to adolescent male violent offending*. Routledge.

Ashton, S. A., & Bussu, A. (2023). The social dynamics of adolescent co-offending. *Youth Justice*, *23*(3), 350–371. https://doi.org/10.1177/14732254221136044

Ashton, S. A., & Ioannou, M. (2022). The relationship between gang membership and psychological risks to offending desistance in a sample of adolescent and young adult males. *Journal of Gang Research*, *29*(2), 29–49. https://www.ngcrc.com/ngcrc/page2.htm

Ashton, S. A., Ioannou, M., & Hammond, L. (2018). Offending patterns of youth gang members and leavers. *Journal of Gang Research*, *25*(2), 29–49. https://eprints.hud.ac.uk/id/eprint/32140/

Ashton, S. A., & Ward, J. (2022). Bridging the gap between criminal psychology and frontline youth work: A case study in programme development and evaluation. In *Assessment & development matters*. The British Psychological Society. https://doi.org/10.53841/bpsadm.2022.14.4.14

Barry, M. (2006). *Youth offending in transition: The search for social recognition*. Routledge. https://doi.org/10.4324/9780203027387

Bolden, C. L. (2012). Liquid soldiers: Fluidity and gang membership. *Deviant Behavior*, *33*(3), 207–222. https://doi.org/10.1080/01639625.2010.548655

Bussu, A., Creaney, S., Price, J., Burns, S., & Myles, K. (2024). 'It's a sixth sense . . . I see you, you see me, and we've been there': Benefits and challenges of developing a peer mentoring scheme with young people in youth justice services. *British Journal of Community Justice*, *19*(2), 4–19. https://doi.org/10.48411/4c2h-hc54

Bussu, A., & Karp, D. (2025). Restorative justice in higher education: An analysis of challenges, strategies, and achievements using Normalization Process Theory. *Innovative Higher Education*, *51*, 293–325. https://doi.org/10.1007/s10755-025-09846-5

Bussu, A., & Karp, D. R. (2026a). Achievements and Challenges with Embedding Restorative Justice in Higher Education: Lessons from Institutional Experiences. *Journal of Criminal Justice Education*, 1–27. https://doi.org/10.1080/10511253.2026.2677152

Bussu, A., & Karp, D. R. (2026b). Institutionalizing restorative justice in higher education: Insights from practitioners. *The Journal of Higher Education*. Advance online publication. https://doi.org/10.1080/00221546.2026.2684839

Bussu, A., Paolini, D., Pulina, M., & Zanzurino, G. (2022). From choice to performance in secondary schools: Evidence from a disadvantaged setting in Italy. *Italian Economic Journal*, *9*(2), 529–555. https://doi.org/10.1007/s40797-021-00178-9

Bussu, A., Veloria, C. N., & Boyes-Watson, C. (2018). StudyCircle: Promoting a restorative student community. *Pedagogy and the Human Sciences*, *6*(1), 1–20. https://scholarworks.merrimack.edu/phs/vol6/iss1/6/

Carson, D. C., Peterson, D., & Esbensen, F. A. (2013). Youth gang desistance: An examination of the effect of different operational definitions of desistance on the motivations, methods, and consequences associated with leaving the gang. *Criminal Justice Review*, *38*(4), 510–534. https://doi.org/10.1177/0734016813511634

Carson, D. C., & Vecchio, J. M. (2015). Leaving the gang: A review and thoughts on future research. In S. H. Decker & D. C. Pyrooz (Eds.), *The Wiley handbook of gangs* (pp. 257–275). Wiley-Blackwell.

Casassa, K., Knight, L., & Mengo, C. (2022). Trauma bonding perspectives from service providers and survivors of sex trafficking: A scoping review. *Trauma, Violence, & Abuse*, *23*(3), 969–984. https://doi.org/10.1177/1524838020985542

County Lines Pathfinder. (2022). *Child criminal exploitation: Safe and effective exit*. Youth Justice Board.

Creaney, S., & Burns, S. (2024). Freedom from symbolic violence? Facilitators and barriers to participatory practices in youth justice. *Youth Justice*, *24*(1), 31–52. https://doi.org/10.1177/14732254231156844

Creaney, S., & Burns, S. (2025). The Achilles heel of child first: High-risk panels in youth justice service policy and practice. *Probation Journal*. Advance online publication. https://doi.org/10.1177/02645505251353719

Creaney, S., Burns, S., Douglas, A.-M., Brierley, A., & Falconer, C. (2024). Desistance through participatory practice: Involving children in decision-making processes in youth justice. In A. Wigzell, C. Paterson-Young, & T. Bateman (Eds.), *Desistance and children: Critical reflections from theory, research and practice* (pp. 212–227). Policy Press. https://doi.org/10.51952/9781447369127.ch011

Creaney, S., Price, J., Bussu, A., Burns, S., & Myles, K. (2026). The social and educational value of peer mentoring in a youth justice context. In A. A. Shafi, H. Kent, S. Case, & N. Hazel (Eds.), *The Palgrave handbook on the education of children in criminal justice settings*. Palgrave Macmillan. https://link.springer.com/book/9783032231192

Darby, B., Barlow, C., Heys, A., & Green, S. (2026). Child criminal exploitation and the victim–offender overlap: A trauma-informed reconceptualisation. *Criminology & Criminal Justice*. Advance online publication. https://doi.org/10.1177/17488958261436596

D'Andrea, W., Ford, J. D., Stolbach, B., Spinazzola, J., & van der Kolk, B. A. (2012). Understanding interpersonal trauma in children: Why we need a developmentally appropriate trauma diagnosis. *American Journal of Orthopsychiatry, 82*(2), 187–200. https://doi.org/10.1111/j.1939-0025.2012.01154.x

Esbensen, F.-A., Huizinga, D., & Weiher, A. H. (1993). Gang and non-gang youth: Differences in explanatory factors. *Journal of Contemporary Criminal Justice, 9*, 94–116. https://doi.org/10.1177/104398629300900203

Farrall, S. (2002). *Rethinking what works with offenders: Probation, social context and desistance from crime*. Willan Publishing.

Farrall, S., Bottoms, A., & Shapland, J. (2010). Social structures and desistance from crime. *European Journal of Criminology, 7*(6), 546–570. https://doi.org/10.1177/1477370810376574

Farrall, S., Hunter, B., Sharpe, G. J., & Calverley, A. (2014). *Criminal careers in transition: The social context of desistance from crime*. Oxford University Press.

Firmin, C. (2020). *Contextual safeguarding and child protection: Rewriting the rules*. Routledge. https://doi.org/10.4324/9780429283314

Haines, K., & Case, S. (2015). *Positive youth justice: Children first, offenders second*. Policy Press. https://doi.org/10.51952/9781447321729

Hesketh, R. F., & Robinson, G. (2019). Grafting: "The boyz" just doing business? Deviant entrepreneurship in street gangs. *Safer Communities, 18*(2), 54–63. https://doi.org/10.1108/SC-05-2019-0016

Home Office. (2023). *Criminal exploitation of children and vulnerable adults: County lines*. https://www.gov.uk/government/publications/criminal-exploitation-of-children-and-vulnerable-adults-county-lines/criminal-exploitation-of-children-and-vulnerable-adults-county-lines

Hopkins, B. (2024). *The role of relational and restorative practice in alternative provision: Reducing violence and overcoming barriers to learning*. Why Me? https://why-me.org/wp-content/uploads/2024/07/The-role-of-relational-and-restorative-practice-in-AP.pdf

Jay, A., Bailey, S., & Geekie, C. (2024). *Shattered lives, stolen futures: The report of the Jay Review of Criminally Exploited Children*. Action for Children. https://www.actionforchildren.org.uk/documents/3290/Shattered_Lives_Stolen_Futures_Report_-_Full_Report.pdf

Laub, J. H., & Sampson, R. J. (2003). *Shared beginnings, divergent lives: Delinquent boys to age 70*. Harvard University Press.

Marshall, H. (2023). Victims first? Examining the place of 'child criminal exploitation' within 'child first' youth justice. *Children & Society, 37*(4), 1156–1170. https://doi.org/10.1111/chso.12696

Marshall, H. (2024). Child criminal exploitation and the interactional emergence of victim status. *The British Journal of Criminology, 64*(5), 1011–1027. https://doi.org/10.1093/bjc/azae008

Maruna, S. (2001). Making good: How ex-convicts reform and rebuild their lives. *American Psychological Association*. https://doi.org/10.1037/10430-000

Maruna, S. (2016). Desistance and restorative justice: It's now or never. *Restorative Justice*, *4*(3), 289–301. https://doi.org/10.1080/20504721.2016.1243853

Maruna, S. (2017). Desistance as a social movement. *Irish Probation Journal*, *14*, 5–20. https://www.probation.ie/EN/PB/0/D0A39BFFC60AB69880258 1D0003CB6D2/$File/ShaddMaruna_IPJarticle.pdf

Maxwell, N. (2023). I'm trying to save my family: Parent experiences of child criminal exploitation. *Youth Justice*, *23*(2), 243–258. https://doi.org/10.1177/14732254221122559

Maxwell, N. (2026). 'Shove that. There's always hope': Young people's lived experience of child criminal exploitation. *Journal of Youth Studies*, *29*(1), 54–70. https://doi.org/10.1080/13676261.2024.2397025

Maxwell, N., Wallace, C., Cummings, A., Bayfield, H., & Morgan, H. (2019). *A systematic map and synthesis review of child criminal exploitation*. Cardiff University. https://orca.cardiff.ac.uk/id/eprint/131950/

McAra, L., & McVie, S. (2010). Youth crime and justice: Key messages from the Edinburgh Study of Youth Transitions and Crime. *Criminology & Criminal Justice*, *10*(2), 179–209. https://doi.org/10.1177/1748895809360971

McNeill, F. (2006). A desistance paradigm for offender management. *Criminology & Criminal Justice*, *6*(1), 39–62. https://doi.org/10.1177/1748895806060666

McNeill, F. (2015). Desistance and criminal justice in Scotland. In H. Croall, G. Mooney, & R. Munro (Eds.), *Crime, justice and society in Scotland* (pp. 200–216). Routledge.

McNeill, F., & Weaver, B. (2010). *Changing lives? Desistance research and offender management*. Scottish Centre for Crime and Justice Research.

Nugent, B., & Schinkel, M. (2016). The pains of desistance. *Criminology & Criminal Justice*, *16*(5), 568–584. https://doi.org/10.1177/1748895816634812

Ogeil, R. P., Cheetham, A., Mooney, A., Allen, N. B., Schwartz, O., Byrne, M. L., . . . & Lubman, D. I. (2019). Early adolescent drinking and cannabis use predicts later sleep-quality problems. *Psychology of Addictive Behaviors*, *33*(3), 266–273. https://doi.org/10.1037/adb0000453

Pyrooz, D. C., & Decker, S. H. (2011). Motives and methods for leaving the gang: Understanding the process of gang desistance. *Journal of Criminal Justice*, *39*(5), 417–425. https://doi.org/10.1016/j.jcrimjus.2011.07.001

Pyrooz, D. C., Decker, S. H., & Webb, V. J. (2010). The ties that bind: Desistance from gangs. *Crime & Delinquency*, *60*(4), 491–516. https://doi.org/10.1177/0011128710372191

Reid, J. A. (2024). Trauma bonding and human trafficking. In J. A. Reid (Ed.), *Trauma bonding and interpersonal crimes* (pp. 81–98). Wiley.

Sanchez, R. V., Speck, P. M., & Patrician, P. A. (2019). A concept analysis of trauma coercive bonding in the commercial sexual exploitation of children. *Journal of Pediatric Nursing*, *46*, 48–54. https://doi.org/10.1016/j.pedn.2019.02.030

Veloria, C. N., Bussu, A., & Murray, M. (2020). The transformative possibilities of restorative approaches to education. In C. Pica-Smith, C. N. Veloria, & R. Contini (Eds.), *Intercultural education: Critical perspectives, pedagogical challenges, and promising practices* (pp. 298–320). Nova Science Publishers.

Weaver, B. (2016). *Offending and desistance: The importance of social relations*. Routledge.
Wigzell, A., & Paterson-Young, C. (2025). *Progressive desistance practice in youth justice*. HM Inspectorate of Probation. https://cdn.websitebuilder.service.justice.gov.uk/uploads/sites/32/2025/05/Academic-Insights-Wigzell-and-Paterson-Young.pdf
Wigzell, A., Paterson-Young, C., & Bateman, T. (Eds.). (2024). *Desistance and children: Critical reflections from theory, research and practice*. Policy Press. https://nectar.northampton.ac.uk/id/eprint/20348/1/Wigzell_et_al_2024_Desistance_and_Children.pdf
Youth Justice Board. (2022a). *Child criminal exploitation: Safe and effective exit*. County Lines Pathfinder Programme. https://yjresourcehub.uk/wp-content/uploads/media/Child_Criminal_Exploitation_Safe_and_Effective_Exit_Briefing_Paper_County_Lines_Pathfinder_2022.pdf
Youth Justice Board. (2022b). *A guide to child first*. Youth Justice Board.

6 Conclusions

Towards a process-oriented understanding of child criminal exploitation

6.1 Conceptualising child criminal exploitation: vulnerability, exploitation, and entrenchment

This book has argued that CCE should not be understood as a discrete criminal event, a singular safeguarding issue, or solely through narrow definitions associated with county lines and modern slavery. Instead, drawing upon the experiences of participants, the empirical evidence presented throughout the book, and existing criminological and psychological literature, the authors have conceptualised CCE as a layered, cumulative, and process-oriented form of exploitation shaped by structural vulnerability, relational coercion, emotional adaptation, trauma, and constrained agency (Barlow et al., 2022; Beckett & Warrington, 2014; Firmin, 2017, 2020).

As discussed throughout Chapters 1–4, children and young people's involvement in CCE cannot be adequately understood through simplistic offender-based frameworks that prioritise criminal choice and individual responsibility while overlooking coercion, manipulation, and institutional failure (Case & Haines, 2015; Marshall, 2023, 2024). Rather than viewing exploitation as a static category of harm, this book has demonstrated that CCE develops progressively across interconnected psychological, social, relational, and structural dimensions that reinforce one another over time.

Chapter 1 established the foundations of the model by examining early vulnerability, safeguarding failures, and constrained choice and are illustrated in Figure 6.1, which conceptualises CCE as a layered process in which institutional failures create the foundations for vulnerability and exploitation. Although the narratives of exploitation varied between participants, they revealed common vulnerabilities and failures. At the foundation of the model are institutional safeguarding failures, including school exclusion, failure to protect children from familial violence and co-offending, professional confusion in recognising the victim–offender overlap, and limited recognition of coercive control (Maxwell et al., 2026).

Insufficient protective services may leave children vulnerable to criminal exploitation. While CCE is often associated primarily with modern slavery and

DOI: 10.4324/9781003496694-7

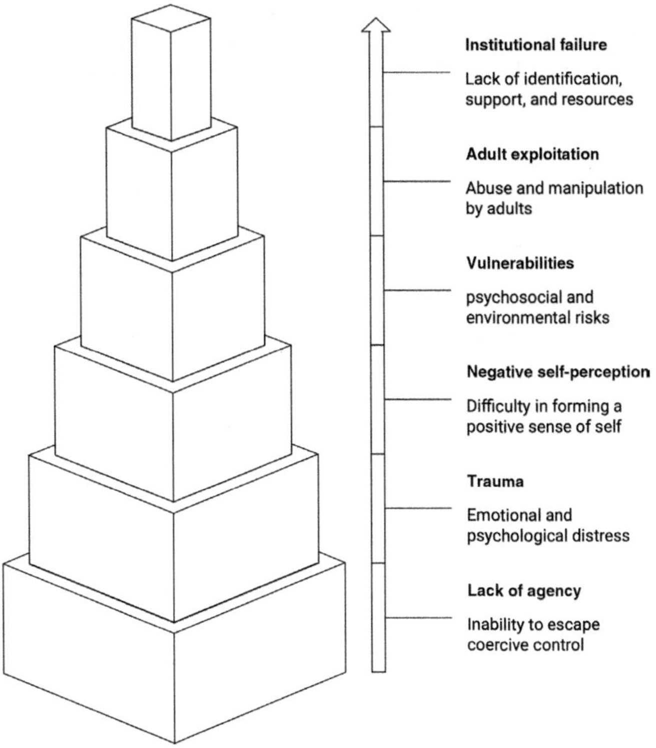

Figure 6.1 Foundations of vulnerability and exploitation

the transportation of drugs out of the area, the findings of this book indicate broader forms of exploitation across a range of income-generating offences outside and typically before involvement with organised criminal groups. The cycle of exploitation may intensify vulnerability before, during, and after the process, meaning that young people require additional support after they have exited the exploitative relationship. Negative self-perception may function either as a risk factor, when group membership is experienced as the only available option, or as a protective factor, when it becomes part of a turning point towards desistance. For those still being exploited, psychological trauma and threats of violence against the young person and their family may produce a perceived lack of agency, which can present as hostility towards professional support.

These experiences subsequently contribute to trauma, negative self-perception, and progressively constrained agency, making disengagement increasingly difficult. The model reflects the cumulative and cyclical nature of exploitation identified throughout participants' narratives. Importantly, the figure demonstrates that exploitation is not simply the result of individual criminality but emerges through the interaction among social environments, relational dynamics, emotional processes, and failures of protection and support.

One of the key arguments advanced in this book is that institutional safeguarding failures frequently form the foundation upon which exploitation develops. Participants repeatedly described experiences of school exclusion, exposure to violence within the family environment, unmet emotional and psychological needs, poverty, unstable home conditions, lack of supportive adult relationships, and inconsistent professional intervention. In many cases, systems failed to recognise the overlap between victimisation and offending, instead responding to exploited children primarily through criminal justice frameworks rather than safeguarding approaches. This reflects wider concerns within the literature regarding the difficulties practitioners experience in recognising coercive control, relational manipulation, and the victim–offender overlap within CCE contexts (Firmin, 2020; Haines & Case, 2015; Marshall, 2023, 2024).

The findings presented throughout the book also suggest that current understandings of CCE remain too narrow. Although public and policy discussions frequently associate CCE with county lines activity and the transportation of drugs across geographical areas, participants described broader forms of exploitation linked to a range of income-generating offences, including acquisitive crime, organised theft, violence, robbery, and group-based offending. The findings therefore support broader conceptualisations of exploitation that move beyond drug distribution models and recognise the diverse ways in which children may be manipulated, controlled, and exploited for criminal purposes.

Importantly, this book has shown that vulnerability should not be understood solely as a pre-existing condition that precedes exploitation. Rather, vulnerability is continuously reproduced throughout the exploitation process itself. Young people often entered exploitative environments with existing adversities and vulnerabilities, including ACEs, exposure to violence, emotional neglect, social exclusion, and poor mental health. However, exploitation further intensifies these vulnerabilities through repeated exposure to trauma, fear, emotional distress, violence, and relational dependency (Barlow et al., 2022; Reid, 2024). In this respect, the cycle of exploitation increases vulnerability before, during, and after exploitation, meaning that young people often require significant long-term support even after disengagement from criminal groups or exploitative relationships.

The role of group processes emerged as another important theme throughout the book. Chapter 2 showed how co-offending, training by older individuals, peer influence, and group loyalty can embed children within exploitative networks. Participants described complex co-offending roles within exploitative groups, including followers, instigators, and those occupying fluid positions across offending hierarchies. Group belonging frequently provided emotional security, protection, identity, and recognition that were absent elsewhere in young people's lives. Older group members often acted as trainers, role models, or authority figures, socialising younger children into offending behaviours and normalising criminal activity over time (Harding, 2020; Robinson et al., 2019). Loyalty to the group was therefore not simply criminal allegiance but often reflected relational dependency, emotional attachment, and survival within environments characterised by violence and instability.

The findings in Chapter 2 have important implications for practice and intervention. Attempts to remove young people from exploitative groups without addressing the emotional, relational, and social functions fulfilled by those groups may have limited success. Participants frequently described "testing" behaviours by exploiters that reinforced fear, dependency, and loyalty. Understanding these relational dynamics is essential for practitioners attempting to identify coercion and exploitation. Trauma-informed approaches may therefore be particularly important, especially when young people appear resistant or hostile towards professional intervention (Day et al., 2023; Malvaso et al., 2024). In many cases, this hostility may reflect fear, manipulation, trauma bonding, or perceived threats towards themselves and their families rather than genuine unwillingness to engage with support.

The emotional dimensions of exploitation and offending also represented a significant contribution of this book. Chapter 3 demonstrated how emotions and create points of rupture that provide opportunities for intervention. It also demonstrated how emotions experienced during crime, after offending, and following arrest play an important role in shaping both continued involvement in exploitation and pathways towards desistance. Participants described a range of emotional experiences, including excitement, belonging, fear, numbness, guilt, shame, and emotional detachment. Importantly, some young people initially experienced involvement in organised criminal groups as exciting or thrilling, particularly where group membership provided status, recognition, or excitement absent elsewhere in their lives. However, over time, these experiences frequently became associated with coercion, oppression, violence, and psychological distress.

The findings suggest that emotional responses represent important opportunities for intervention and prevention. Negative emotional reactions following offending, violence, or arrest may function as rupture points, increasing self-awareness and openness to support (Giordano et al., 2002; Maruna, 2001). Equally, neutral emotional responses and emotional desensitisation may reflect the normalisation of exploitation and violence. Interventions should therefore focus not only on behaviour but also on emotional awareness, emotional processing, and helping young people critically to reflect critically on their experiences. Supporting emotional recognition may strengthen protective factors and increase young people's ability to recognise coercion, manipulation, and exploitation within their relationships and environments.

The role of identity and self-perception also emerged strongly throughout the book and was the focus of *Chapter 4* with respect to group entrenchment. Participants frequently described low self-esteem, feelings of inadequacy, and limited future aspirations prior to exploitation. For some young people, membership within organised criminal groups provided a sense of identity, purpose, belonging, and status that was unavailable elsewhere. However, negative self-perception also appeared to function as both a risk factor and, in some cases, a protective factor. While some participants felt trapped within deviant identities and believed criminal group membership represented their only realistic pathway, others described moments of self-reflection that contributed towards desistance and disengagement. This highlights the importance of identity transformation within the desistance process and supports wider desistance literature emphasising the role of recognition, belonging, and identity reconstruction (Maruna, 2001; Weaver, 2016).

6.2 Desistance, constrained agency, and recovery

One of the most important arguments advanced throughout this book concerns the limitations of traditional desistance models when applied to CCE and was explored in detail in Chapter 5. Conventional desistance theories frequently assume levels of agency, rational choice, and voluntary disengagement that may not be available to children who are being criminally exploited. Even when a young person escapes or disengages from an exploitative group, this does not necessarily mean that they have desisted from crime altogether. Some young people may continue individual offending because they have acquired criminal skills, developed greater autonomy, remain affected by financial need, or continue to seek excitement, status, or belonging outside the group context. This finding is consistent with international literature on gang membership and offending (Ashton & Ioannou, 2022; Pyrooz et al., 2014). Desistance from the group, therefore, should not be conflated with desistance from offending behaviour. This distinction is critical for practitioners, as removal from exploitation represents only the first stage of a longer process of recovery, identity reconstruction, and social reintegration.

This book has therefore conceptualised release from CCE as a conditional and situationally mediated process rather than a purely voluntary withdrawal from crime. Opportunities for disengagement emerge when harmful relational networks are disrupted and when young people are provided with realistic alternatives, relational safety, emotional support, and sustained institutional intervention. Some participants described continuing individual offending activities after leaving organised criminal groups, particularly offences associated with thrill-seeking, excitement, or financial survival. Young people may possess offending skills, autonomy, and criminal training acquired during exploitation that continue beyond group disengagement. This further highlights the limitations of simplistic binary distinctions between "in exploitation" and "desisted". The authors suggest that the process consists of "in exploitation", "release from coercive control", and "desistance from offending behaviours" (Figure 6.2).

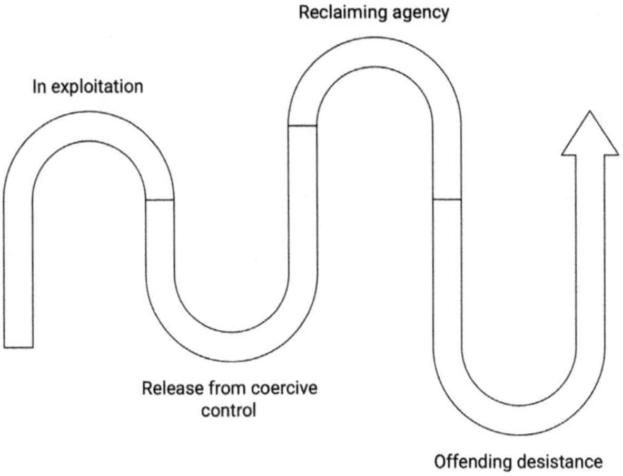

Figure 6.2 Child criminal exploitation desistance model

The findings also demonstrate that removal from exploitation should be understood as only the first stage of recovery. Escaping an exploitative relationship or criminal group does not automatically resolve trauma, emotional distress, fear, or social vulnerability. Young people frequently require substantial long-term support following exploitation, including psychological intervention, educational reintegration, relational support, stable housing, financial assistance, and opportunities for positive identity development (Darby et al., 2026; Office for Health Improvement and Disparities, 2022; Taggart, 2018). Without such support, vulnerabilities may persist and increase the risk of re-exploitation or continued offending.

6.3 Implications for policy, practice, and future research

These findings have important implications for policy and practice. Responses to CCE should move beyond punitive and offender-focused frameworks and instead prioritise safeguarding (Firmin, 2017, 2020), trauma-informed practice, contextual safeguarding approaches, and long-term relational intervention. Schools and educational settings are particularly important within this process. As discussed in Chapters 4 and 5, restorative and relational approaches within educational settings may strengthen belonging, reduce exclusion, and provide young people with alternative sources of identity, recognition, and support (Bussu et al., 2018; Veloria et al., 2020). This is particularly significant given the strong links among school exclusion, social marginalisation, and vulnerability to exploitation identified throughout participants' narratives.

Relational and restorative approaches may also support longer-term disengagement and recovery by creating opportunities for accountability, dialogue, relational repair, and reintegration, provided such interventions remain voluntary, trauma-informed, and attentive to victims' safety and needs (Bussu & Karp, 2025; Bussu & Karp, 2026). More broadly, the findings highlight the importance of *training* professionals across education, social care, youth justice, policing, and safeguarding se*rvices to recognise coercion, trauma, emotional manipulation, and the victim–offender overlap within CCE contexts.* Failure to recognise these dynamics risks further criminalising exploited children and reinforcing cycles of harm.

Professional training should therefore move beyond narrow criminal justice understandings of exploitation and instead equip practitioners to recognise relational coercion, trauma responses, emotional manipulation, group dynamics, and constrained agency within children's narratives and behaviours. Improving professional understanding of these processes may support earlier identification, reduce inappropriate criminalisation, and strengthen safeguarding responses across agencies (Maxwell et al., 2025).

Several limitations should also be acknowledged. The study draws primarily upon retrospective participant narratives, which may be influenced by memory reconstruction and post hoc interpretation. The sample size limits broader generalisation, and future research would benefit from larger and more diverse samples, including greater exploration of gendered experiences, cultural differences, and longitudinal pathways through exploitation and desistance. Further research is also needed to evaluate the effectiveness of trauma-informed, relational, and restorative interventions specifically designed for children affected by CCE.

Ultimately, this book has argued that children involved in CCE should not be understood solely through the lens of offending but through the intersecting realities of vulnerability, coercion, trauma, emotional adaptation, and survival (Barlow et al., 2022; Firmin, 2020; Marshall, 2024). By conceptualising exploitation as a layered and cumulative process rather than a singular criminal event, this book offers a framework capable of integrating psychological, criminological, and safeguarding perspectives. Sustainable desistance from exploitation, therefore, depends not only upon individual change but also upon whether children are provided with protection, recognition, relational safety, and realistic alternatives capable of interrupting cycles of exploitation and harm.

References

Ashton, S. A., & Ioannou, M. (2022). The relationship between gang membership and psychological risks to offending desistance in a sample of adolescent and young adult males. *Journal of Gang Research*, *29*(2), 1–25. https://www.ngcrc.com/journal.html

Barlow, C., Kidd, A., Green, S. T., & Darby, B. (2022). Circles of analysis: A systemic model of child criminal exploitation. *Journal of Children's Services, 17*(3), 158–174. https://doi.org/10.1108/JCS-04-2021-0016

Beckett, H., & Warrington, C. (2014). *Suffering in silence: Children and unreported crime*. University of Bedfordshire.

Bussu, A., & Karp, D. (2025). Restorative justice in higher education: An analysis of challenges, strategies, and achievements using Normalization Process Theory. *Innovative Higher Education, 51*, 293–325. https://doi.org/10.1007/s10755-025-09846-5

Bussu, A., & Karp, D. (2026). Achievements and challenges in embedding restorative justice in higher education: Lessons from institutional experiences. *Journal of Criminal Justice Education*. Advance online publication. https://doi.org/10.1080/10511253.2026.2677152

Bussu, A., Veloria, C. N., & Boyes-Watson, C. (2018). StudyCircle: Promoting a restorative student community. *Pedagogy and the Human Sciences, 6*(1), 1–20. https://scholarworks.merrimack.edu/phs/vol6/iss1/6/

Darby, B., Barlow, C., Heys, A., & Green, S. (2026). Child criminal exploitation and the victim–offender overlap: A trauma-informed reconceptualisation. *Criminology & Criminal Justice*. Advance online publication. https://doi.org/10.1177/17488958261436596

Day, A., Malvaso, C., Boyd, C., Hawkins, K., & Pilkington, R. (2023). The effectiveness of trauma-informed youth justice: A discussion and review. *Frontiers in Psychology, 14*, Article 1157695. https://doi.org/10.3389/fpsyg.2023.1157695

Firmin, C. (2017). *Contextual safeguarding: An overview of the operational, strategic and conceptual framework*. University of Bedfordshire. https://tce.researchinpractice.org.uk/wp-content/uploads/2020/02/Contextual-Safeguarding-An-overview-of-the-operational-strategic-and-conceptual-framework.pdf

Firmin, C. (2020). *Contextual safeguarding and child protection: Rewriting the rules*. Routledge.

Giordano, P. C., Cernkovich, S. A., & Rudolph, J. L. (2002). Gender, crime, and desistance: Toward a theory of cognitive transformation. *American Journal of Sociology, 107*(4), 990–1064. https://doi.org/10.1086/343191

Haines, K., & Case, S. (2015). *Positive youth justice: Children first, offenders second*. Policy Press. https://doi.org/10.51952/9781447321729

Harding, S. (2020). *County lines: Exploitation and drug dealing among urban street gangs*. Bristol University Press.

Malvaso, C. G., Day, A., & Boyd, C. M. (2024). The outcomes of trauma-informed practice in youth justice: An umbrella review. *Journal of Child & Adolescent Trauma, 17*, 939–955. https://doi.org/10.1007/s40653-024-00634-5

Marshall, H. (2023). Victims first? Examining the place of 'child criminal exploitation' within 'child first' youth justice. *Children & Society, 37*(4), 1156–1170. https://doi.org/10.1111/chso.12696

Marshall, H. (2024). Child criminal exploitation and the interactional emergence of victim status. *The British Journal of Criminology, 64*(5), 1011–1027. https://doi.org/10.1093/bjc/azae008

Maruna, S. (2001). *Making good: How ex-convicts reform and rebuild their lives*. American Psychological Association. https://doi.org/10.1037/10430-000

Maxwell, N., Ablitt, J., Davies, B., Hopkinson, M., & Smith, P. (2025). *Complex Safeguarding Wales practitioner toolkit*. Cardiff University. https://www.cardiff.ac.uk/documents/2821101-complex-safeguarding-wales-practitioner-toolkit

Maxwell, N., Khurana, K., & Cserző, D. (2026). 'They're not seeing young people as victims': Professional perspectives on policy and practice for criminally exploited children in Wales. *Youth Justice*, *0*(0). https://journals.sagepub.com/doi/10.1177/14732254261428267

Office for Health Improvement and Disparities. (2022). *Working definition of trauma-informed practice*. GOV.UK. https://www.gov.uk/government/publications/working-definition-of-trauma-informed-practice/working-definition-of-trauma-informed-practice

Pyrooz, D. C., Decker, S. H., & Webb, V. J. (2014). The ties that bind: Desistance from gangs. *Crime & Delinquency*, *60*(4), 491–516. https://doi.org/10.1177/0011128710372191

Robinson, G., McLean, R., & Densley, J. (2019). Working county lines: Child criminal exploitation and illicit drug dealing in Glasgow and Merseyside. *International Journal of Offender Therapy and Comparative Criminology*, *63*(5), 694–711. https://doi.org/10.1177/0306624X18806742

Taggart, D. (2018). *Trauma-informed approaches with young people: Frontline briefing*. Research in Practice. https://www.researchinpractice.org.uk/children/publications/2018/august/trauma-informed-approaches-with-young-people-frontline-briefing-2018/

Veloria, C. N., Bussu, A., & Murry, M. (2020). The transformative possibilities of restorative approaches to education. In C. Pica-Smith, C. N. Veloria, & R. Contini (Eds.), *Intercultural education: Critical perspectives, pedagogical challenges, and promising practices* (pp. 298–320). Nova Science Publishers.

Weaver, B. (2016). *Offending and desistance: The importance of social relations*. Routledge.

Index

Note: page numbers in **bold** indicate a table and page numbers in *italics* indicate a figure on the corresponding page.

For Product Safety Concerns and Information please contact our EU representative GPSR@taylorandfrancis.com Taylor & Francis Verlag GmbH, Kaufingerstraße 24, 80331 München, Germany

Batch number: 10816012

Printed by Printforce, the Netherlands